Floral Design and Blossom

Floral Design and Blossom

CREATIVE & AUTHENTIC FLAIR WITH AN EASY APPROACH TO FLORAL DESIGNING

M. C. S. Antoniou

ANCF, LCGI

First published in Great Britain in 2021

Editing, design, typesetting and publishing by UK Book Publishing

www.ukbookpublishing.com

ISBN: 978-1-914195-26-6

Contents

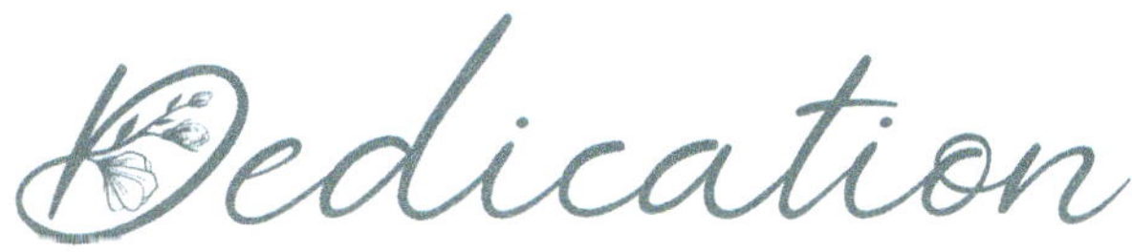

With endless cups of tea, papers, photos all over the table and hardly any breaks while writing this book, choosing lots of special designs, for a new and challenging project that had been on the horizon for some time. This has come into being with the unlimited support and understanding from my family.

So, I thank my husband & family for their support and encouragement for this book to be produced and written and also a special thank you to all family & friends that trusted me to deliver your vision and celebration décor.

With love always xxxx

Acknowledgements

With this book I give great credit to the tutors and floral persons I have met and worked with over the years of learning and working and supporting in the industry.

Thank you, to all, for the skills I have learnt, that I can teach onto others.

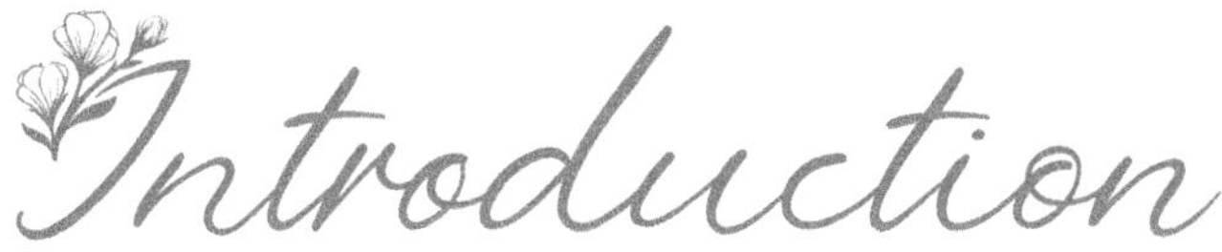

Introduction

HAVING CHANGED CAREERS A FEW YEARS AGO, I wanted to be able to create designs and give inspiration to others. With this in mind, I was aiming to be at a degree level of workmanship and knowledge. I enrolled on several floristry courses and have not looked back, with continuous learning in knowledge and skills, and learning from the best in the industry.

Additionally, being a part of The Chelsea Flower shows on several occasions to represent the colleges and industry bodies alike, as well as meeting like for like people in the commercial floricultural and horticultural industry, from the buyers to the growers, and excellent knowledge of industry supplying organisations in The Netherlands.

Developing further into the floricultural and Horticultural industry has given me a great sense of pride and to be proud. I wanted to be able to deliver great creative designs and experiment further with skills and understanding of the concepts of floristry and garden designing and develop in an inspirational way. This also gave me more inspiration to develop further in the Horticultural industry with additional learning in Garden Design that gave me a more accurate understanding of gardens and their needs for the individual person needs or projects.

Being able to design contemporary or bespoke bridal bouquet or event décor, gives great rewards.

I also found that learning floristry allows you to grow your own personality. Learning to understand the complications of situations from installations in small events and controlling more commercial designing to coincide with current trends.

The book has a varied selection of floristry workshops for you to 'Have a go' and develop at your own pace for beginners and experienced florists.

With detailed steps to assist you with the making of your chosen designs, there is some alternative options for some designs. All designs can be changed to suit your flower produce that you prefer, by making sure that the sizes of the flowers are similar.

I have had great pleasure in writing this very informative book of floristry workshops, knowledge and learning, and I hope you will enjoy reading it as well as having the confidence to do a workshop, as much as I have writing and producing the book

Enjoy!

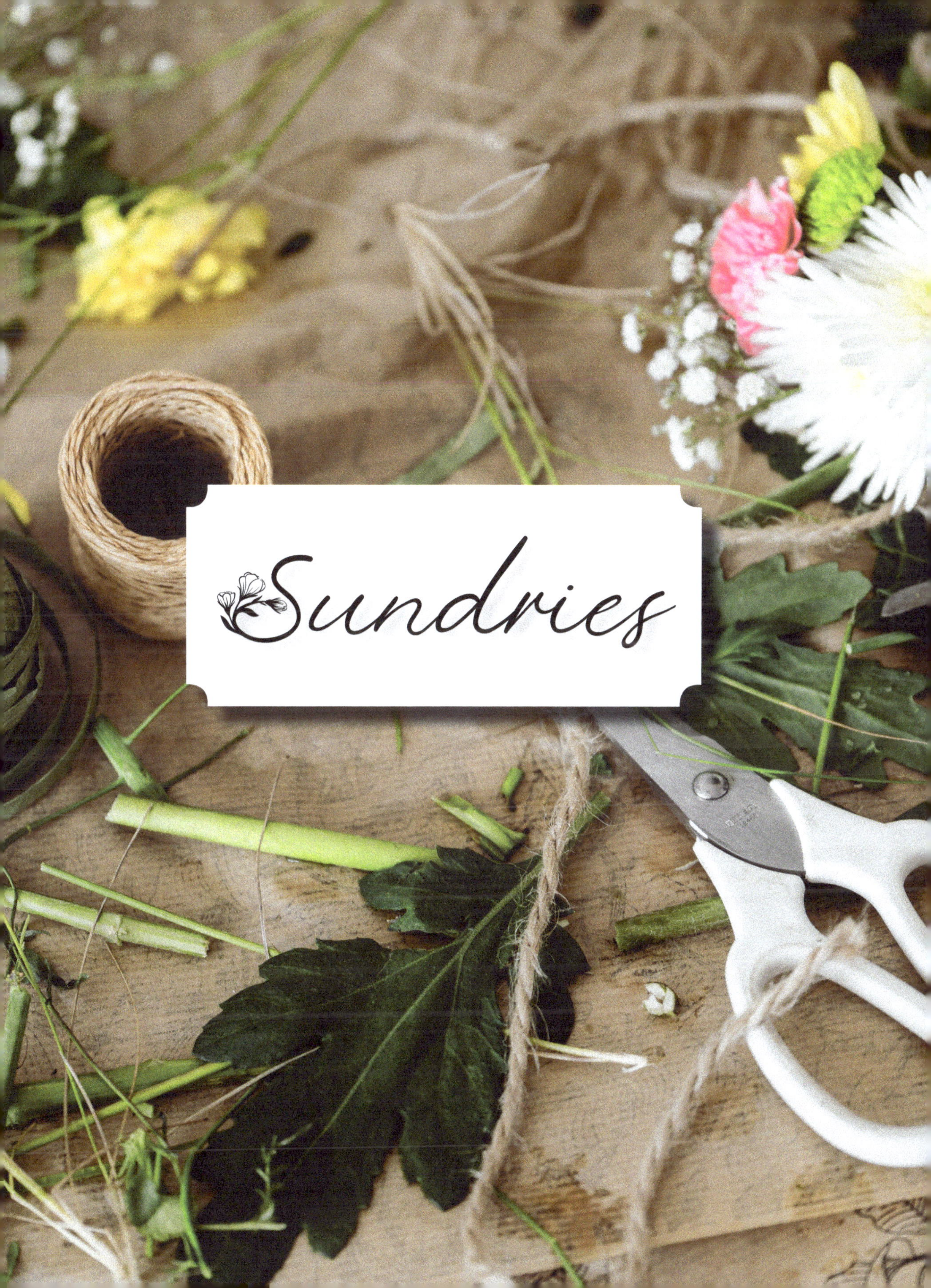
Sundries

Tray sundries

TOP LAYER

- ❑ Large long rectangle low tray
- ❑ Small low bowl (within the tray)
- ❑ Small 'O' bowl (within the tray, with an area for the wet oasis to sit in, this is standard for a centrepiece)
- ❑ A small bridal holder

BOTTOM LAYER FROM THE RIGHT

- ❑ Large pedestal round bowl
- ❑ Medium blue planter bowl (within the bowl)
- ❑ Small rectangular low tray (this fits 1 whole standard block of wet oasis)
- ❑ Medium clear arrangement bowl.

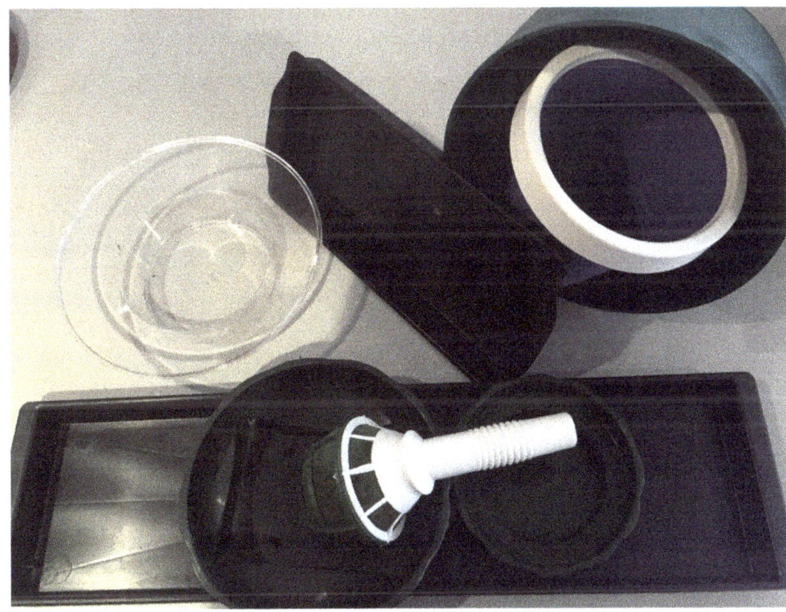

Tray sundries

Decorative accessories

TOP LAYER GOING RIGHT

- ❑ Grey binding wire reel
- ❑ Green binding wire reel
- ❑ Decorative design wire reel on wood. Various colours
- ❑ Fine design wire (gold reel)
- ❑ Fine design wire (purple reel)
- ❑ Thick design wire (silver)
- ❑ Large ended gold and pink pins
- ❑ Set of various size needles
- ❑ Glass stones

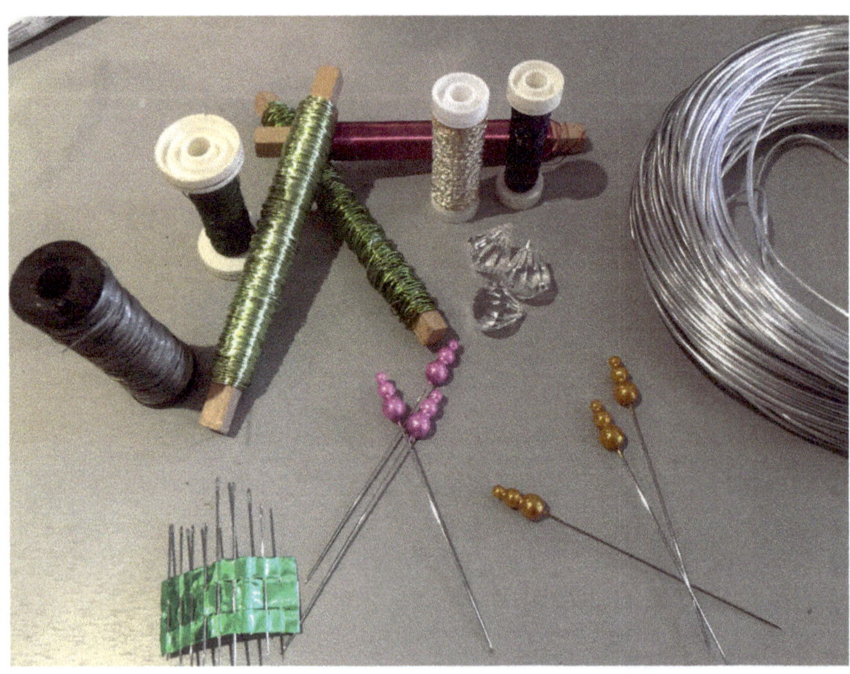

Decorative accessories

Wire gauge sizes

WIRE GAUGE	THICKNESS (IN MILLIMETRES)	USES IN FLORAL ARRANGEMENT
20-Gauge	0.81 mm	Used on harder-stemmed flowers
22-Gauge	0.71 mm	All-purpose wire
24-Gauge	0.56 mm	All-purpose wire
26-Gauge	0.46 mm	All-purpose wire
	0.32. mm	Delicate flowers

WIRED TECHNIQUES

Various wiring techniques can be used for e.g. roses, gerbera, chrysanthemums, carnations, phalaenopsis, cymbidium, dendrobium, salal leaf, ivy leaves, laurel, blue spruce pine and various other fresh produce.

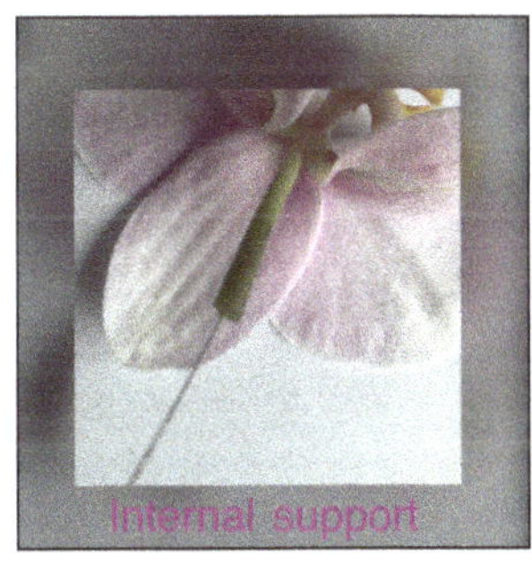

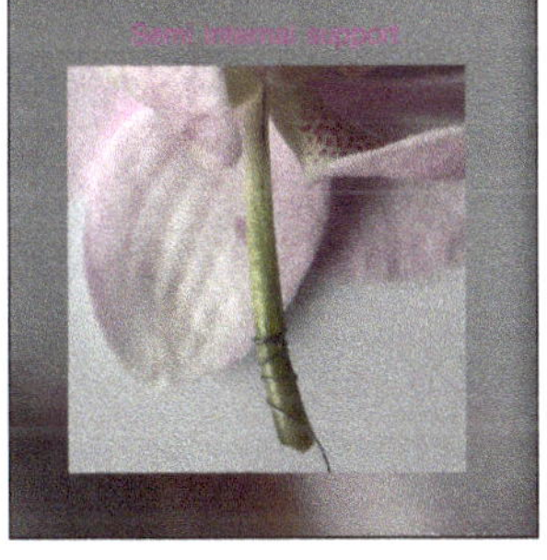

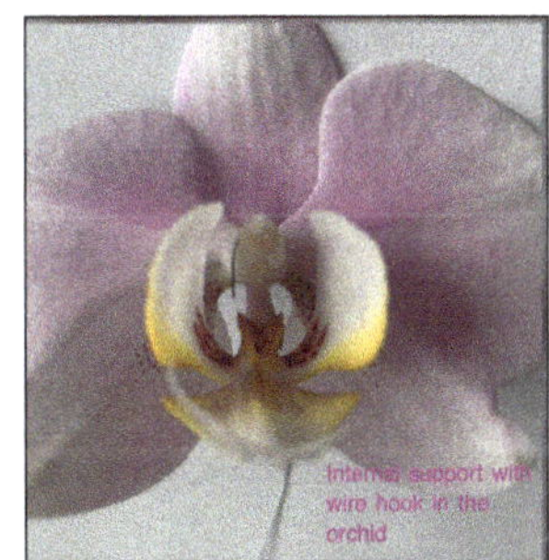

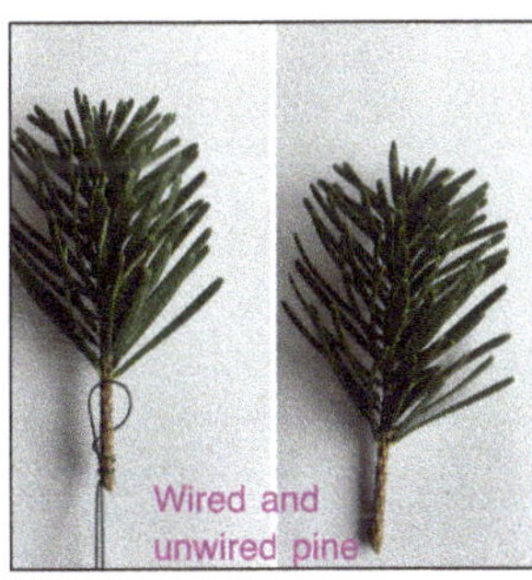

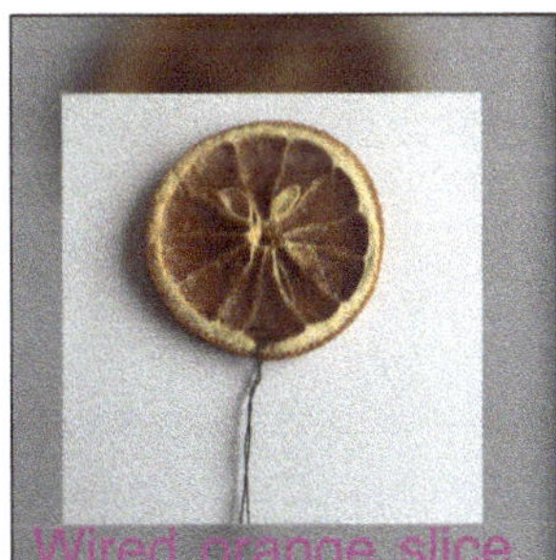

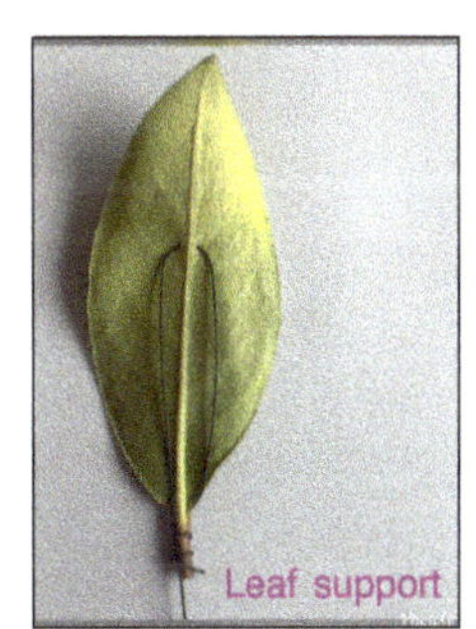

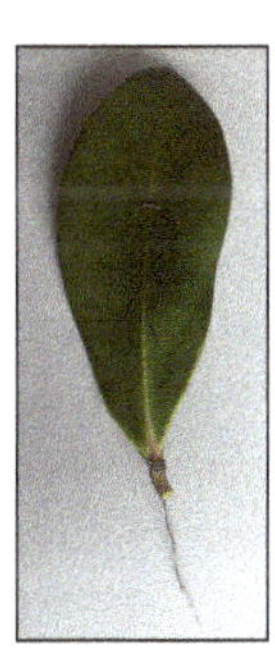

Wire and sundries

FROM CLOCKWISE

- ❑ Wrist corsage band
- ❑ Measuring tape
- ❑ Small green frog leg
- ❑ Large green frog leg
- ❑ Yellow rose thorn cleaner

MIDDLE LAYER

- ❑ Tube of 32 gauge wire
- ❑ Loose 56 gauge wire
- ❑ Tube 71 gauge wire

BOTTOM LAYER

- ❑ Flower food
- ❑ Large flower stem vials
- ❑ Small flower stem vials
- ❑ Florist glue (in a tube)
- ❑ Electric glue gun
- ❑ Glue stick
- ❑ Glue sundries

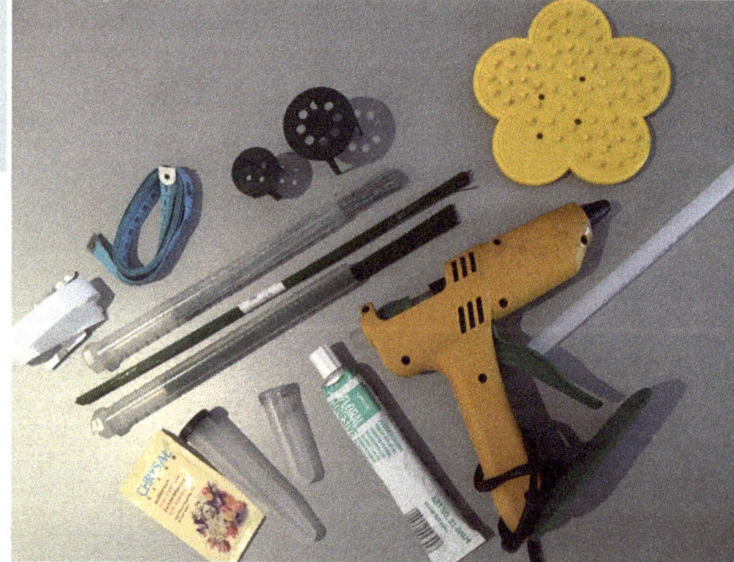

Mechanics

Tapes and sundries

TOP LAYER (STARTING CLOCKWISE)

- ❑ Binding string
- ❑ Oasis fix (this is green and similar texture to Blu Tack)
- ❑ Clear florist tape
- ❑ Green florist tape
- ❑ White stemtex tape (smooth finish)
- ❑ White stemtex (basic)
- ❑ Green stemtex (basic)

MIDDLE LAYER

- ❑ Standard block of wet oasis foam (that can be cut into 3 equal sizes)
- ❑ Small German pins (otherwise known as mossing pins)
- ❑ Large German pins (otherwise known as mossing pins)
- ❑ Mini wire pins (made by bending 56 wire gauge)
- ❑ Medium wire pins
- ❑ Large wire pins (made by bending 71 wire gauge)

BOTTOM LAYER

- ❑ Packed samples of stemtex (sold in retail stores)

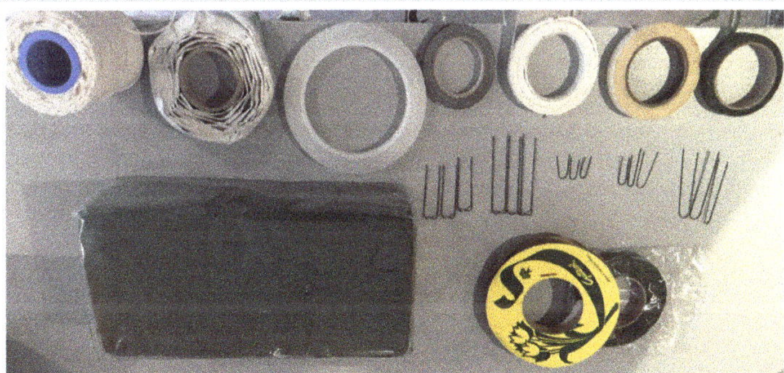

Tape and pin sundries

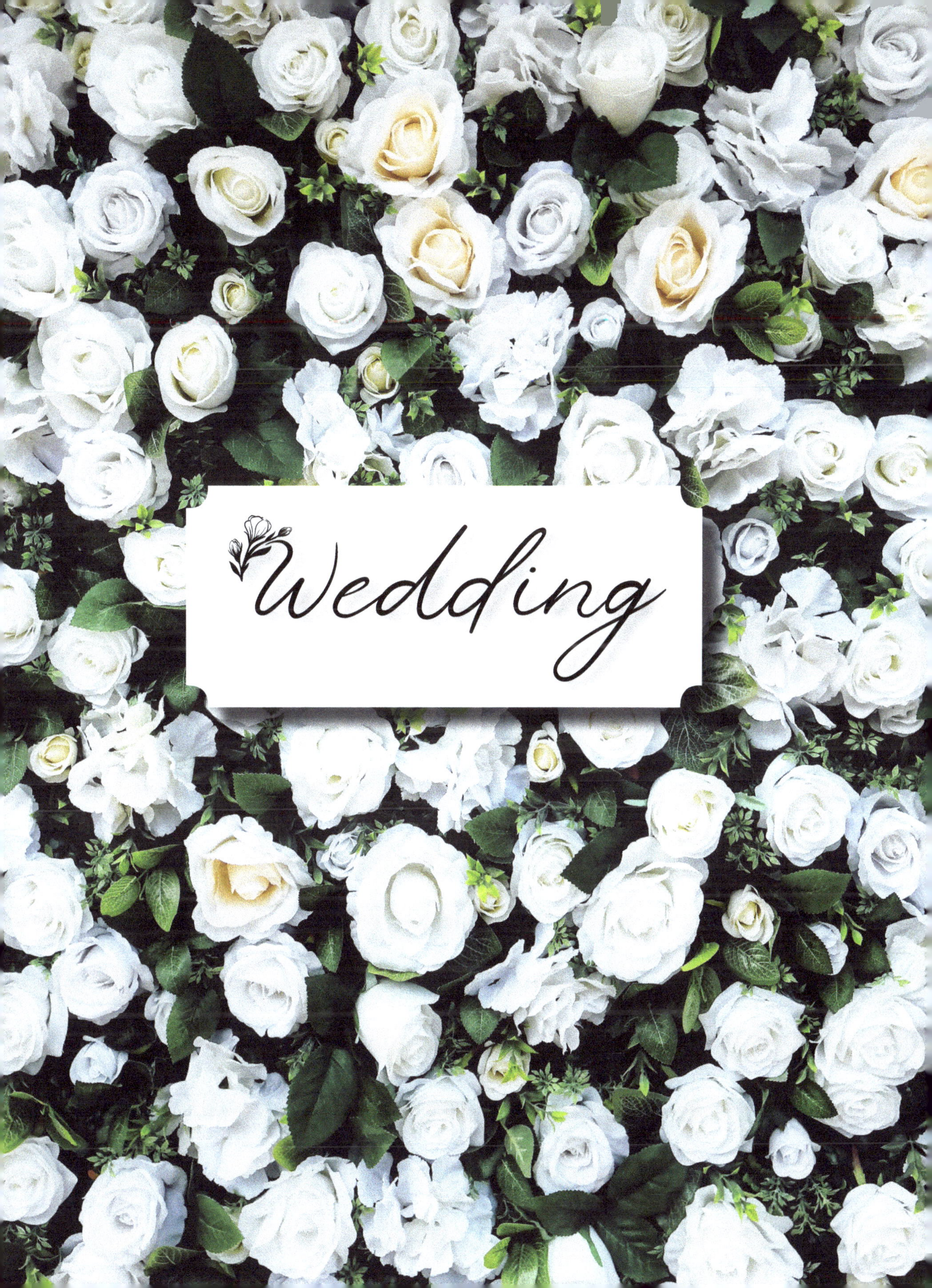
Wedding

Rose and Orchid Bouquet

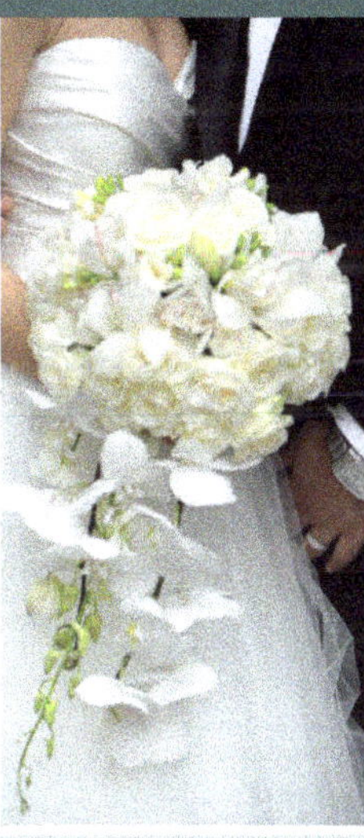
Rose and orchid bouquet

PRODUCE

- ❑ 80 white akito roses cut to 6 to 8 inches
- ❑ 4 stems dendrobium orchids
- ❑ 3 stems of phalaenopsis orchids
- ❑ 2 stems of white freesias cut into 10 inches
- ❑ 1 stem of white cymbidium orchids cut into 10 inches

SUNDRIES

- ❑ 1 medium bridal bouquet holder (soaked in a bucket of water)
- ❑ 74 wire (for 10 to 20 wired roses)
- ❑ 56 gauge wire for the cymbidium
- ❑ Florist tape

METHOD

1. Cut and wire your roses to 6 to 8 inches.
2. Cut the remaining roses to size also.
3. Apply the wired roses in first on the perimeter (you may need to wire more roses).
4. Once perimeter is done add another row round the bouquet.
5. Working inwards.
6. Wire the cymbidium orchids (florets) separately with care leaving some wire free to insert into oasis well (2 to 3 inches).
7. Add the cymbidium orchids into the bouquet working inside the circle of roses.
8. Next row of roses.
9. Finish off with orchids.
10. And you may need to place a rose in the centre.
11. Add your freesias in balanced areas.
12. Place the phalaenopsis orchids underneath the bouquet (wire the stem first).
13. And push firmly in 2½ inches in.
14. Place the other phalaenopsis orchid next to the first one (cut to a smaller length) the same way.
15. And the other side of the longer phalaenopsis orchid the same.
16. Add the smaller stems of phalaenopsis within the bottom third of the bouquet, in between the roses and aim downwards to the floor while inserting the orchids, holding the handle in position as the bride would be holding it.
17. (optional) Tape the bottom of the bouquet with tape and cover the handle with ribbon and your crystal beads on the fine design wire for some shine.

Alternative flowers can be used • Refer to wiring techniques

18. Present to the bride.

Gentlemen's corsage

PRODUCE

- ❑ 1 or 2 stem dendrobium orchid

SUNDRIES

- ❑ 32 wire gauge (1)
- ❑ Green/ white florist stemtex tape to bind
- ❑ 1 buttonhole pin

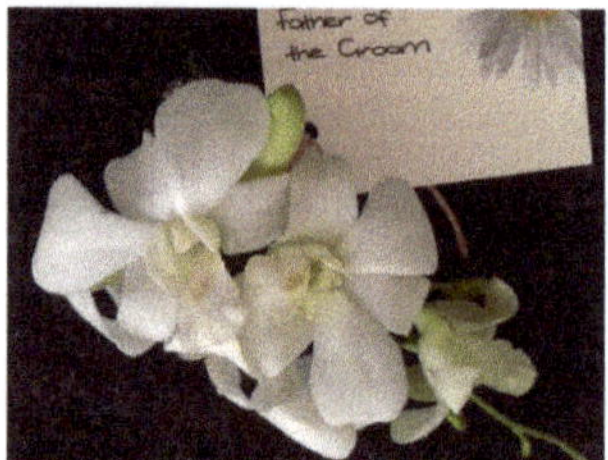

Hand / wrist corsage

METHOD

1. Cut the top of the dendrobium orchid to 3 buds. Leave to one side.
2. Cut a dendrobium orchid off the rest of the stem and prepare for wiring.
3. Gently put the 32 gauge wire through the central part in the dendrobium and giving a gentle push it should pierce through to the top stem (joining the flower).
4. Pull through about 3 inches gently, so as not to break the dendrobium orchid.
5. Gently bend the wire and wind it round to include the other part of the wire, by twisting the wire round the flower stem (1 or 2 turns) as high to the flower as you can.
6. Cover the wire to 1 inch down.
7. Continue to do this for another 4 open dendrobium buds.

CONSTRUCTION

8. Hold the first stem you cut.
9. Apply the second bloom to the left, slightly below the semi open bloom on the first stem.
10. Add the second bloom to the right, holding firmly in place.
11. Finish off by adding the 3rd bloom in the middle, by bending the wire slightly so you have it facing you with the stems all together.
12. Cut the stems to 1½ inches, still holding firmly, and start to tape firmly with the stemtex tape.
13. Continue to tape to the bottom and allow a slight fold at the very bottom of the stems.
14. Apply a pin at an angle - ready for groomsman.

Wedding, christening and engagement events • Alternative flowers can be used • Refer to wiring techniques

Wrist corsage

PRODUCE

- ❑ 2 blooms of phalaenopsis orchids

FOLIAGE

- ❑ 1 small stem of soft ruscus

SUNDRIES

- ❑ 1 wrist thin bangle
- ❑ 32 gauge wire for the phalaenopsis
- ❑ Stemtex (white) for binding

METHOD

1. Wire the phalaenopsis carefully by making a very tiny fold at the top of the 32 wire, 2½ mm loop at the top end of the 32 wire.
2. Thread this through the orchid carefully not to break the stem.
3. Pull the wire down and until the loop pulls back or feels firmly in place and leave some free wire to bind at the bottom
4. Wire the soft Ruscus by twisting the 32 gauge wire around the stem of 1½ inch.
5. Tape well with stemtex.
6. Join the ruscus with the phalaenopsis orchids and bind well with stemtex, and cover and secure well the 1½ inch stem.
7. Bend the wrist corsage slightly to attach to the wrist bangle (this bit a bit fiddly) but make sure it is completely secured to the bangle.
8. (You may need to tape some stemtex around the bangle also.)

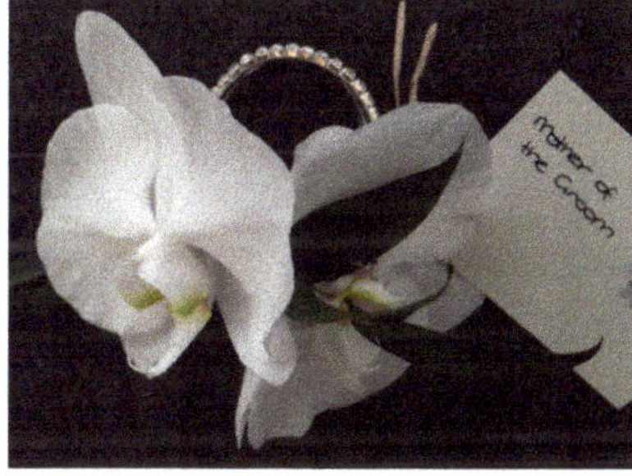

Hand / wrist corsage

Place on wrist - can be used for proms, weddings, parties and Valentine's • Alternative flowers can be used • Refer to wiring techniques

Ranunculus posy

PRODUCE

- ❑ 15 to 20 ranunculus stems conditioned with low level leaves removed and ends to stems cut neatly

SUNDRIES

- ❑ 1 whole retail reel of design wire 2mm thickness (turquoise) - you will need about 1½ metres approx
- ❑ ½ whole retail reel of design wire 2mm thickness (pink) - you will need about 1 metre approx.
- ❑ ½ a retail reel of thick rope 5mm approx
- ❑ Some stem tape to secure all the stems together

METHOD

1. Hold all the ranunculus in one hand lightly.
2. With your other hand tidy the stems, so they are all regimented and facing down neatly
3. Then apply the stem tape by placing it at the top (from about 2 to 3 inches down from the blooms) and start to twist and turn as you bind the stems with the tape.
4. Continue this for a few turns and then slightly aim vertically to add a secondary layer.
5. The stem should be covered (½ to ¾ inch in thickness) with the tape.
6. Adding the design wire to the bouquet first (pink design wire).
7. Attach 1 inch into the stems from underneath.
8. Start to loosen the wire and wind around the ranunculus bloom. This will create a collar for the ranunculus to sit on.
9. Add the (turquoise) design wire by the same method and wind down, this time around the stem, trying to keep the wire in place and connected to the last wind (refer to picture).
10. Secure both wire ends to the bouquet by placing into a safe part of the bouquet (in this case the stems).

11. Attach the rope by placing into the design wire carefully and secure with a small pin (facing down on inserting into stems).
12. Continue to wind round the stem ¼ way down, and secure with a pin inserting upwards into the stem.

Present to a guest • Alternative flowers can be used

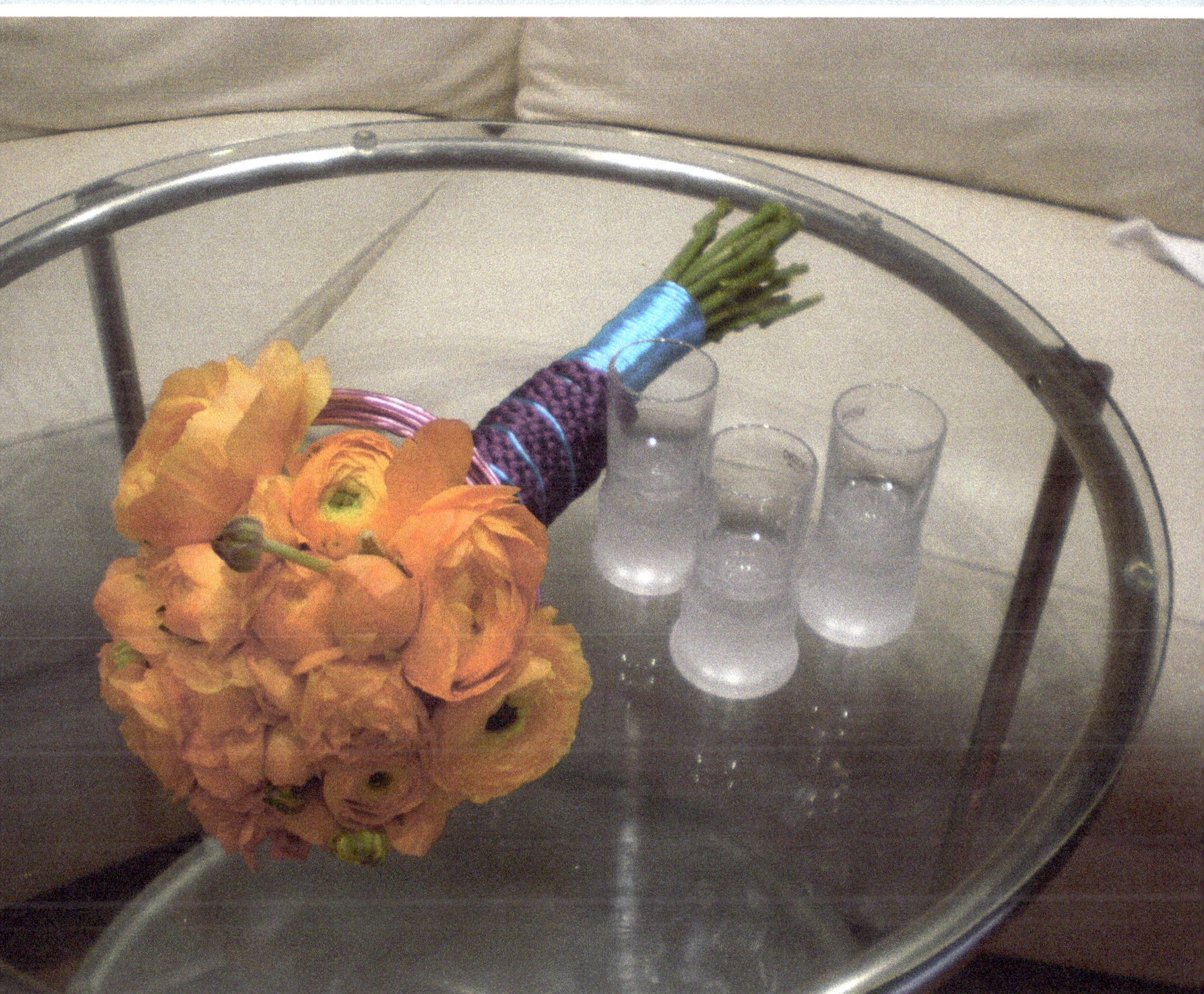

Ranunculus bouquet / posy

Hand posy - Techniques. Banding, Grouping

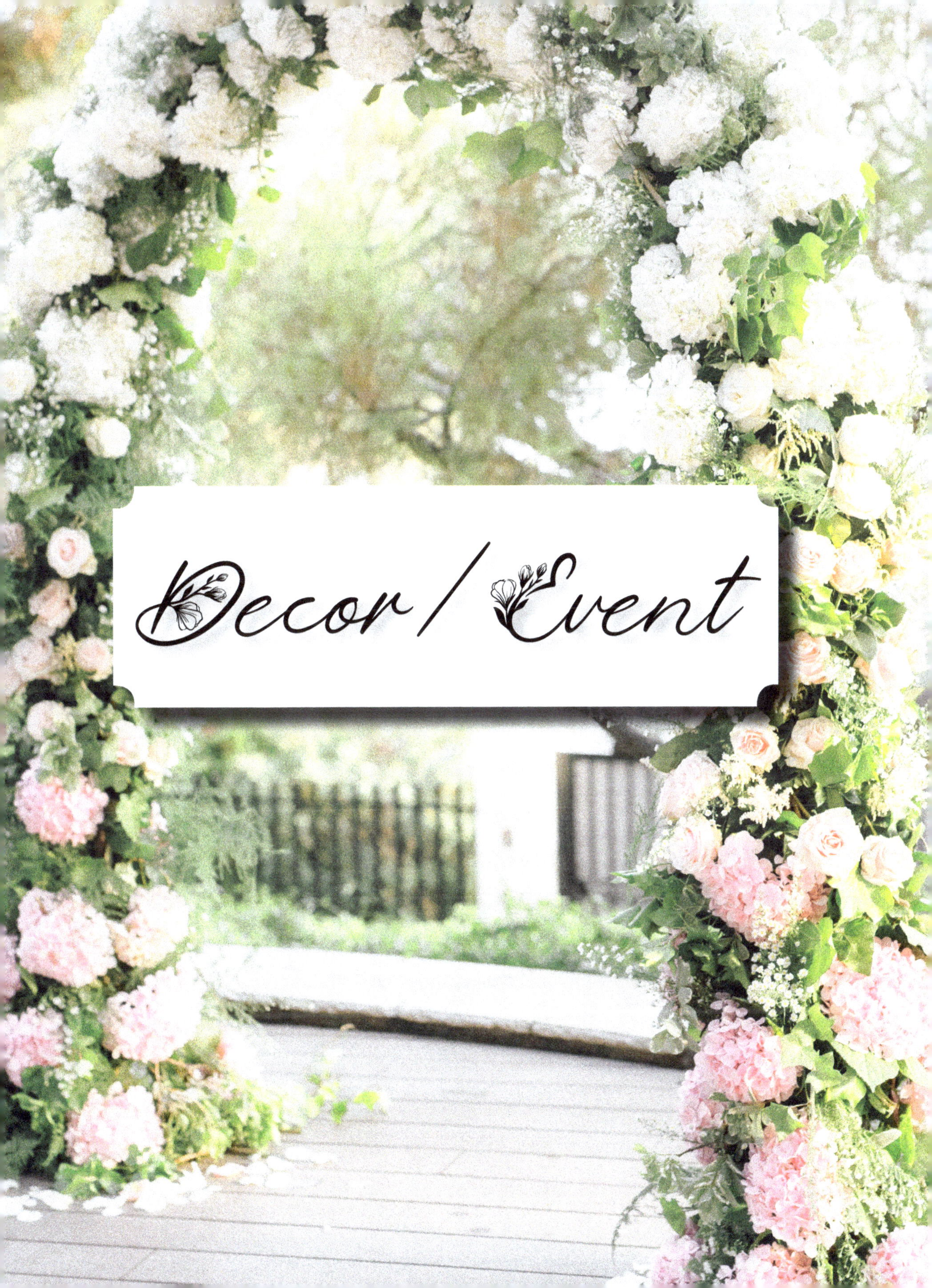
Decor / Event

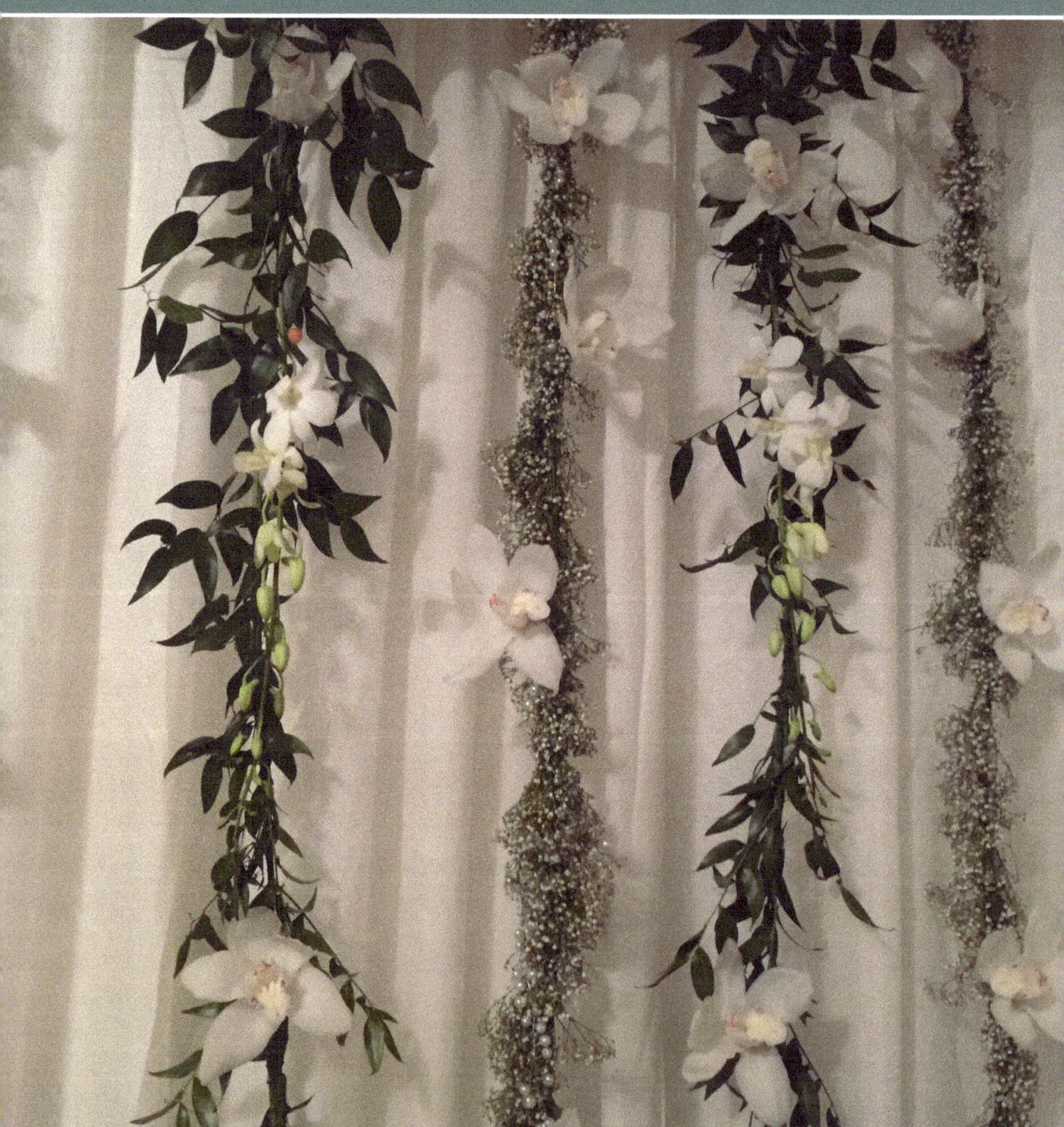

Vertical Garlands

Garland backdrop

PRODUCE

To make 3 garlands approximately 1½m in length

- ❑ 6 stems gypsophila
- ❑ 6 stems soft ruscus
- ❑ 6 stems dendrobium orchids
- ❑ 9 loose orchids (possibly you will need 3 full stems)

SUNDRIES

- ❑ Binding wire on a reel

METHOD

1. Join 1 stem ruscus to another ruscus from the bottom of the stem.
2. Add the tip of the second ruscus to it and bind with binding wire, about 2 inches up, twisting round a few times until secure.
3. Do this 3 times, then set 3 ruscus garlands aside. Refer to image and Christmas garland.
4. For the gypsophila, the same method, but using the cut stems (6 to 8 inches).
5. Apply one flower stem to another so it is fuller. Wire and twist; do not cut the wire!
6. Continue to add the gypsophila just below the previous one and wind with wire a few times. Continue this method until you have 1½ metres of garland (to match the ruscus).
7. Do this 3 times, set garlands aside.
8. Take the ruscus garland and apply wire to the top stem, by taking a 74 wire gauge and using the same wire and twisting method, apply the wire half way across the stem and twist round both a few times. Leaving 4 inches to make a hook.
9. This to attach to the marquee poles under the pelmet.

CONSTRUCTION/ INSTALLATION

10. Apply the garlands to the marquee poles, by placing the leftover wire under the main pole and bringing over to twist onto the main stem of the garland (should you need a longer wire, add an extension of 74 wire gauge to the binding part of the stem and secure it well). (Additionally, you may need assistance here and a small step ladder - and health and safety procedures.)
11. Do this 5 more times for the rest of the garlands.
12. Gently attach the dendrobium that is in a water vial to the garland, giving each garland an equal amount of space to hang. With the reel wire attach and secure to the ruscus garlands.
13. Apply the orchids (once Stemtexed) equally in the same way to the gypsophila garlands.
14. Space out the garlands equally amongst the marquee area you are working on.

Design can be used for small institutions on walls, windows and windowsills • Alternative flowers and foliage can be used • Refer to wiring techniques and Christmas garland techniques and image.

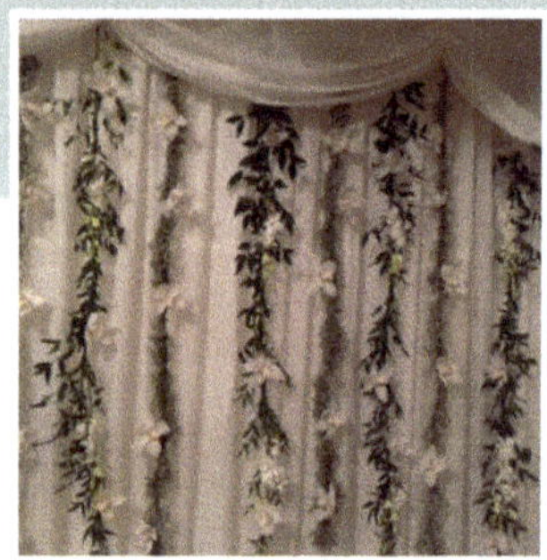

Garland

Techniques, Feathering, mirroring, taping, threading, knotting, winding

Staircase handle decor

PRODUCE

- ❑ 7 dendrobium stems
- ❑ 11 cymbidium orchids

FOLIAGE

- ❑ 4 long soft ruscus stems
- ❑ 2 long eucalyptus stems (baby blue)

SUNDRIES

- ❑ Reel wire to join the ruscus together and the eucalyptus (garland)
- ❑ Stemtex tape for orchids
- ❑ Clear florist tape to attach garland to staircase banister
- ❑ 1 small Le bump (for the banister handle)
- ❑ 7 small water vials for the dendrobium

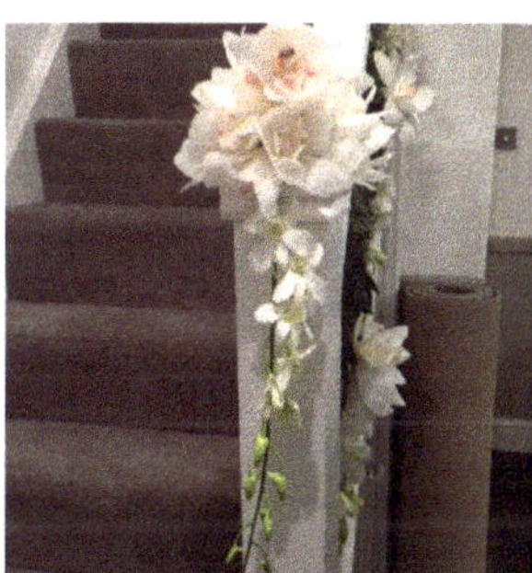

Dendrobium staircase and handle decor

METHOD

1. Start to join the ends of the ruscus to the eucalyptus with the reel wire, twisting round several time to feel secure.
2. Then secure the garland to the staircase with the clear florist tape, keeping this as tidy as possible.
3. With the dendrobium in the water vial, place in position on the garland (you may need assistance here) under the foliage a bit so as not to show.
4. Using some cut reel wire, twist the reel wire around the vial and add it to the garland at the same time, leaving some wire to attach to the spindle for added security.
5. Additionally this will hide the vial.
6. Cut the orchids individually and tape with stemtex (to hold the water moisture in) and attach them each to 1 dendrobium by wiring to the top of the whole dendrobium stem (you may need to go under the dendrobium here. (Refer to picture.)
7. Soak the Le-bump.
8. Remove sticky film, attach to stair handle (centrally).
9. Add the cymbidium (to Le bump, not forgetting to wire them first).
10. Then add the dendrobium facing down in front of the banister handle. (Refer to picture.)

Alternative flowers can be used • Refer to wiring techniques

Staircase decor

PRODUCE

- ❑ 7 dendrobium stems
- ❑ 11 cymbidium orchids cut into 6 inches

FOLIAGE

- ❑ 4 long soft ruscus stems
- ❑ 2 long eucalyptus stems (baby blue)

SUNDRIES

- ❑ Reel wire to join the ruscus together and the eucalyptus (garland)
- ❑ Stemtex tape for orchids
- ❑ Clear florist tape to attach garland to staircase banister
- ❑ 1 small Le-bump (for the banister handle)
- ❑ 7 small water vials for the dendrobium

METHOD

1. Start to join the ends of the ruscus to the eucalyptus with the reel wire, twisting round several times to feel secure.
2. Then secure the garland to the staircase with the clear florist tape, keeping this as tidy as possible.
3. With the dendrobium in the water vial, place in position on the garland (you may need assistance here) under the foliage a bit so as not to show.
4. Using some cut reel wire, twist the reel wire around the vial and add it to the garland, at the same time leaving some wire to attach to the spindle for added security.
5. Additionally this will hide the vial.
6. Cut the cymbidium orchids with the full length of the flower stem individually and tape with stemtex (to hold the water moisture in) and attach them each to 1 dendrobium by wiring to the top of the whole dendrobium stem (you may need to go under the dendrobium here) (refer to image).

7. Soak the Le-bump.
8. Remove sticky film, attach to stair handle (centrally).
9. Add the cymbidium to the Le bump not forgetting to wire them first).
10. Then add the dendrobium facing down in front of the banister handle (refer to image).

Can be extended in quantity lengths to suit a longer staircase • Alternative flowers and foliage can be used • Refer to wiring techniques

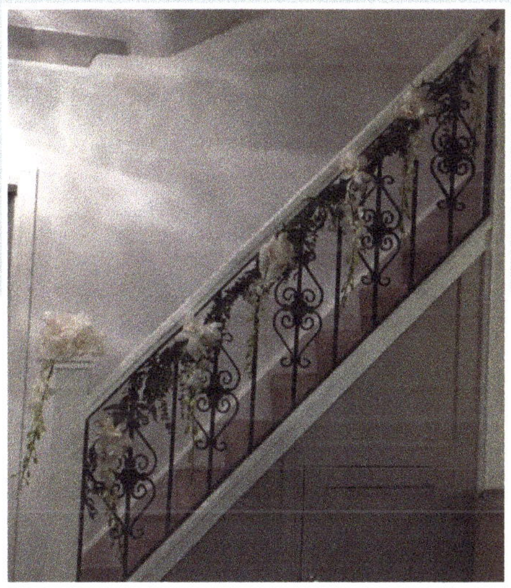

Dendrobium staircase

Suitable for any event or party

Small party sphere

PRODUCE

- ❑ 25 dianthus (carnations)

FOLIAGE

- ❑ 1 stem variegated euonymus

SUNDRIES

- ❑ 1 tall square or round glass vase
- ❑ 1 mini tray (for wet oasis)
- ❑ ¼ block wet oasis
- ❑ Florist tape to bind the oasis to the bowl
- ❑ 1 small frog's leg to fasten the oasis to the mini bowl
- ❑ ¼ inch oasis fix to fasten the frog's leg to the mini bowl
- ❑ Beads

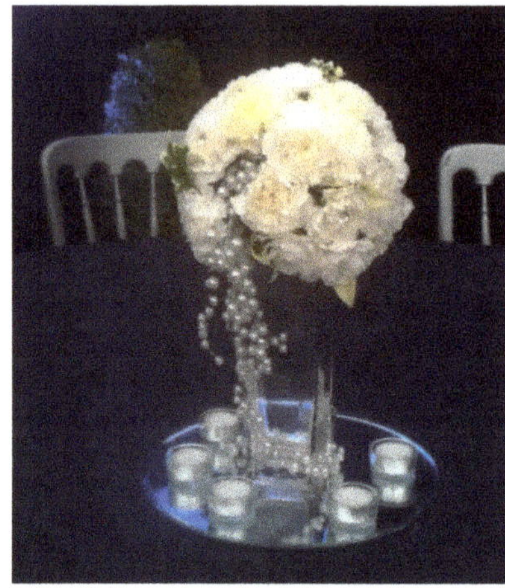

Party Sphere

METHOD

1. Soak oasis.
2. Pop a little of oasis fix ¼ inch to the central part of the mini bowl.
3. Apply frog's leg to it, pressing firmly down.
4. Place the wet oasis on to it, keeping it central.
5. Tape over the bowl and oasis with florist tape to secure in place.
6. Start by cutting the carnations to 6 inches.
7. Place one in at 1½ inches into the sphere.
8. Continue in this manner until the whole sphere has been covered.
9. Evenly place small stems of euonymus to fill any gaps.
10. Apply your beads (to your design).

Place on event table with additional mirror and candles if desired
• Alternative flowers can be used

Fireplace decor

PRODUCE

- ❑ 30 tulips

FOLIAGE

- ❑ 15 long twigs

SUNDRIES

- ❑ 1 long low small tray
- ❑ 1 block of wet oasis
- ❑ Florist tape
- ❑ 1 to 2 metres chicken wire
- ❑ Large moss pins

METHOD

1. Place the wet oasis on the tray and tape up.
2. Place the chicken wire over the whole tray leaving 3 to 4 inches around the perimeter of the whole tray. (You're creating a bubble effect over the oasis tray.) Be careful here.
3. Using the moss pins, with care place the chicken wire and secure with the pins to the oasis.
4. Continue to go round the oasis tray in this manner, making sure the chicken wire is firmly secured.

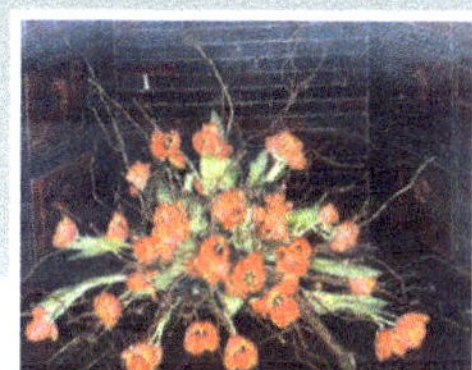

Fireplace decor

CONSTRUCTION

5. Apply the tulips to the oasis through the chicken wire at various lengths and covering the whole area.
6. Allow the tulips to behave naturally. Making sure the mechanics are well covered.
7. Add the twigs evenly and in a natural way.

Place in a fireplace or can be displayed for a corporate function as a focal design • Alternative orange and red flowers can be used • Health and safety practice adhered to.

Church aisle decor

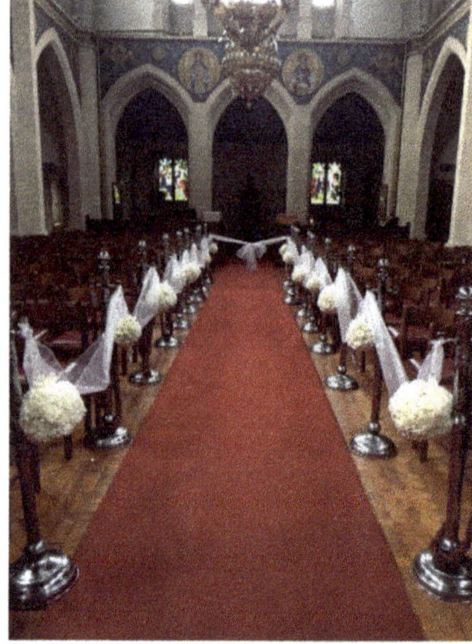

Church aisle

PRODUCE

- ❑ 7 small sphere flower balls with chrysanthemum (you will need 5 full stem spray chrysanthemums)
- ❑ 7 small sphere flower balls with carnations (you will need 25 stems carnations)

ADDITIONAL FLOWERS

- ❑ 1 Cymbidium orchid per sphere ball (you may need to wire each bloom with 32 gauge wire), refer to wiring techniques and image on aisle and party piece design.

SUNDRIES

- ❑ 12 to 20 metres of bridal netting (depends how long the aisle is)
- ❑ Pack of transparent elastic to attach netting to pew ends.

INSULATIONS

1. Apply the bridal netting from the front of the aisle pew end.
2. And work up looping a bit as you go.
3. Attach the bride netting to the pew with the elastic.
4. Continue to do this for as many pews you require.
5. (To join the cuts of the bridal netting, try to balance this to a pew end and add extra elastic to secure well.)
6. With a new roll of bridal netting, continue the method on the other side of the aisle.
7. At the end of the aisle join the 2 ends of the netting and make a bow to your preferred size.
8. Cut to size the excess netting.

This will give exclusive access just for the bride and groom

Pomanders

PRODUCE

- ❑ 9 white roses
- ❑ 5 pink dianthus (carnations)
- ❑ 3 stems pink spray carnations

FOLIAGE

- ❑ 1 stem ruscus (small leaf)
- ❑ 1 stem eucalyptus (parvi)
- ❑ 1 stem ruscus (large leaf)

SUNDRIES

- ❑ 1 medium wet oasis sphere ball

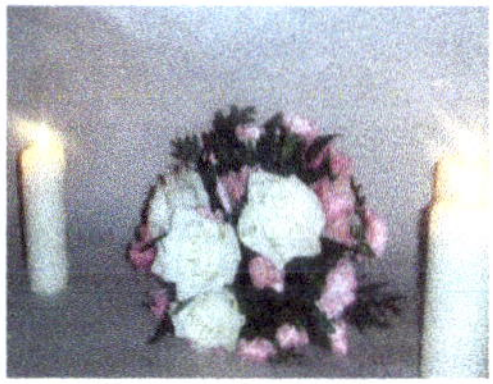

Loose sphere ball

METHOD

1. Wet oasis ball in large bucket full of water, allow to soak water naturally.
2. Remove from bowl and allow to stand for a few minutes.
3. Place oasis ball onto a circular tall vase for support, while you design the sphere.
4. Condition the roses, dianthus and carnations, by removing all leaves.
5. Cut the roses, dianthus to approx 6 inches.
6. Cut the foliage to 6 inches, from the stem, and do not discard the rest; it will be used as filling in gaps.
7. Start with the 6 inch foliage large ruscus and place into oasis ball equally around, pushing the foliage stems into oasis about 1 to 2 inches.
8. Apply the roses. And dianthus in the same way.
9. Add the spray carnations in between the roses & dianthus keeping the shape well compacted.
10. Apply the rest of the ruscus and fill the gaps with the small ruscus cut into 6 inches.

Should you decide to display by hanging on pew ends (reference to image of church aisle), add the looped ribbon though the sphere with 74 wire attached to the ends, and push the wire, right through to the other end and secure well. Then add your flower material.

Alternative flowers can be used and refer to party piece sphere for length of flowers • Refer to wiring techniques

Floaters

PRODUCE

- ❑ 1 or 2 full stems of phalaenopsis orchid
- ❑ 1 full stem of gypsophila
- ❑ Water

SUNDRIES

- ❑ 1 tall clear glass vase
- ❑ 1 medium white or clear pebble about 2 inches wide
- ❑ 1 to 3 floating white or cream candles

METHOD

1. Cut base of stems of orchid and the gypsophila straight to required length.
2. Arrange them with the orchids facing forward, distributing the gypsophila evenly.
3. Arrange the orchids in between the gypsophila.
4. Using the 56 gauge wire, tie all the stems at the base well.
5. Tie the middle and the top of the design with 2 to 6 inches of 32 gauge wire (use as much as you need to fasten the stems well).
6. Attach the stems with a white elastic band to the pebble.
7. Pop the design in the vase.
8. Add water very slowly to start and fill to desired height.
9. With your floating candle, apply gently to your design.
10. Light candle (with health and safety procedure in place).

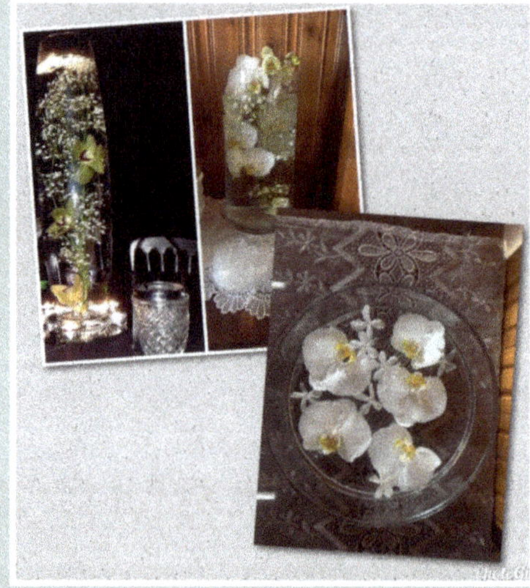

Floaters

Position on focal table • Alternative flowers can be used, as well as vase sizes • Refer to wiring techniques

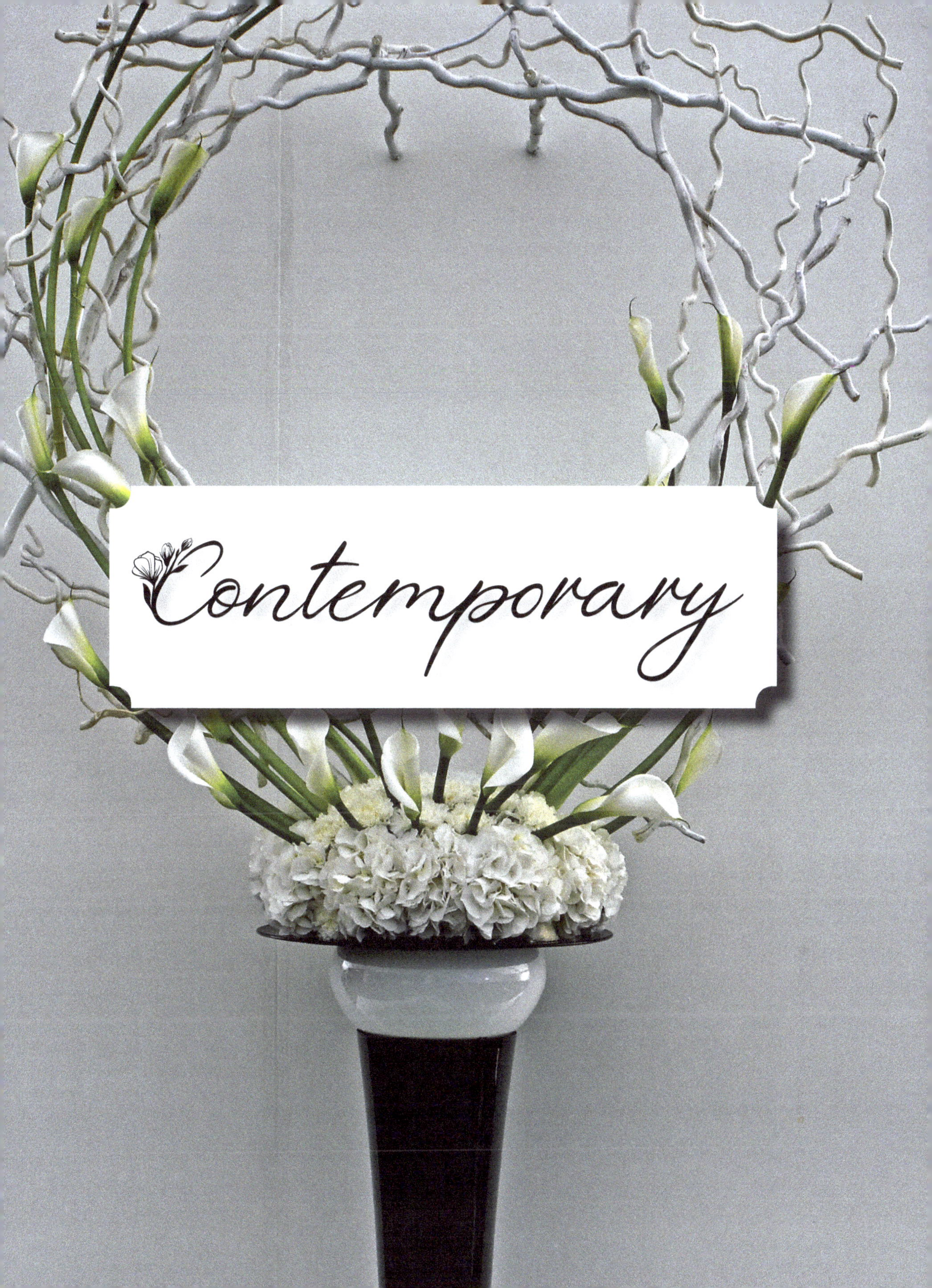
Contemporary

Horizontal display

PRODUCE CUT TO DESIRED LENGTH

5 stems spray carnations
3 stems foxglove
3 anthurium

FOLIAGE

- ❑ 4 phormium leaves
- ❑ 1 medium to large laurel stem, cut in half and stems cut to medium lengths (6 to 8 inches)
- ❑ 6 to 7 large ivy leaves
- ❑ 1 bundle of bear grass (about 20 to 30 stems)
- ❑ ¼ bundle steel grass (10 to 15 stems)
- ❑ 1 stem eucalyptus
- ❑ 2 stems dogwood (cut to various long lengths)
- ❑ 1 stem asparagus fern
- ❑ 1 prayer plant leaf

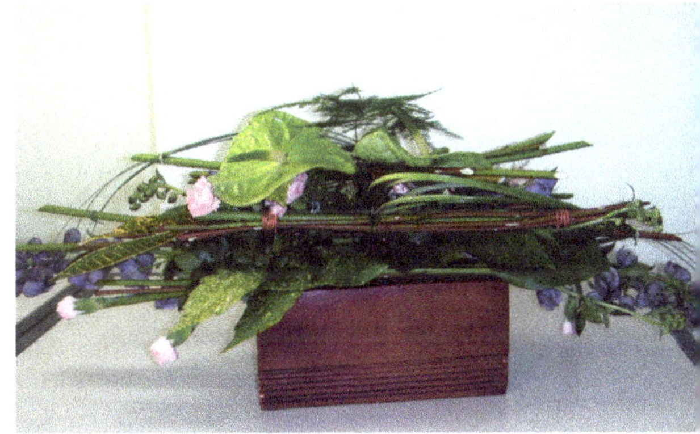

Horizontal design

SUNDRIES

- ❑ * choose one OPTION A or B

A - ⅔ wet oasis blocks placed vertically into container and tape in place.*

Or

B - 1 wet oasis block*

- ❑ 1 long low small tray
- ❑ Florist tape
- ❑ Fine design wire for binding
- ❑ Design wire for binding (decorative)

*The above illustrated design was done with option B**

CONSTRUCTION METHOD

1. Apply wet and ready oasis to the tray.
2. Tape securely with florist tape in 3 equal parts across the whole block vertically.
3. Start with the foliage of laurel, by placing in horizontally, one section to each end.
4. Place your stems of eucalyptus in the same manner in various parts, this in a horizontal fashion. Additionally, the rest of your foliage produce. You can also have a few stems placed facing you (vertically) should you need to for the back.
5. With a few stems of dogwood, bind in an uneven way with the decorative binding wire, leaving 2 to 3 inches of design wire for anchorage into the oasis; place this vertically into the oasis, in the front middle section facing you
6. Apply your carnations up the middle part of the oasis, at the ends placing them firmly in.
7. Continue to add your materials in this way, cutting to size to fit the design, and arrange all round the container. Raising the placements slightly as you go.
8. Add your anthurium at the top central in the oasis, and the fern in the middle of the anthurium, facing toward you
9. Place the bear grass in stems of 3 or 4 and bind the bear grass together with the dogwood, with binding wire.
10. Take 2 stems of steel grass and place in the middle of the design, bending to the left or right, and join them with the dogwood and bind. This is the weaved effect in the illustration.
11. Continue to use this method of binding the dogwood with the bear grass and steel grass, until you are satisfied it's enough.

Place on a corporate reception desktop or focal point to a table setting
• Alternative flowers can be used • Refer to image

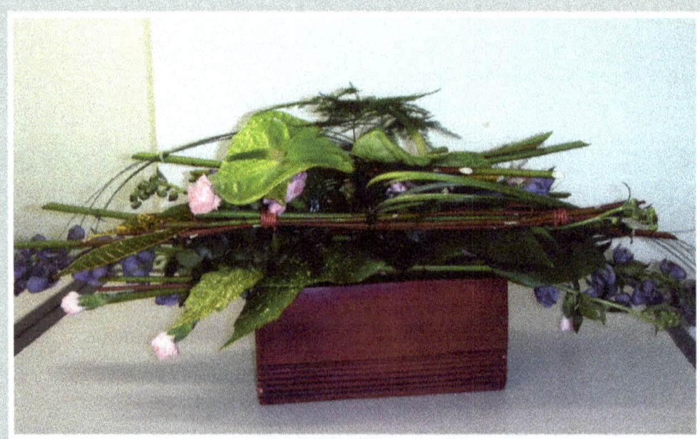

Techniques. Banding, graduating, layering

Contemporary zig zag

PRODUCE

- ❑ 3 snake grass
- ❑ 4 craspedia cut to 12 inches
- ❑ 2 anthurium
- ❑ 3 carnations
- ❑ 2 stems hypericum (you need the berries)
- ❑ 1 stem chrysanthemum (Kermit)

FOLIAGE

- ❑ 3 large variegated ivy leaves
- ❑ Moss for filling gaps
- ❑ ¼ stem eucalyptus (baby blue)

SUNDRIES

- ❑ Colour headed pins
- ❑ 1 square tray (on the same lines as illustration)
- ❑ ¼ block wet oasis
- ❑ 1 small frog's leg
- ❑ 1 inch oasis fix

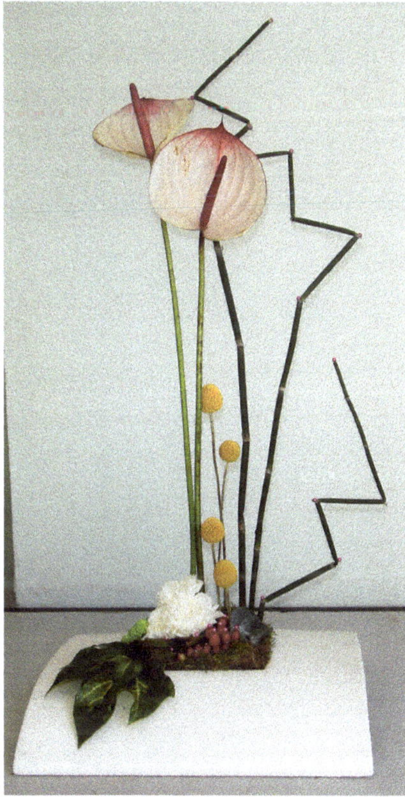

Contemporary Zig Zag Linear

METHOD

1. Wet oasis and allow to rest for a few minutes.
2. Place oasis fix to frog's leg, install the frog to the base of the tray, pushing firmly down.
3. Place wet oasis to the frog leg pushing gently and with a gentle firmness so it's fully in place in the tray.
4. Remove about ⅓ off, or until it's got 1 inch above the tray.
5. Start by placing anthurium in the oasis (back central position).
6. Then the craspedia next to it and then the snake grass.
7. Cut the carnations stem (3 inches) and place in a group together in front of the anthurium and craspedia.

8. Apply the ivy leaves vertically across the display.
9. Apply the hypericum (cut into 2 inches) in a group next to the carnations at a slight angle.
10. Place the chrysanthemum (Kermit cut into 2 inches) into the design in front of the snake grass in a row.
11. Fill the gaps with moss.
12. Gently bend the end one of the snake grass at its nodes and place a coloured headed pin inside. Continue to do the rest at your discretion as to how many you would like.

Place in a prominent position - suitable for reception desktops
• Alternative flowers can be used

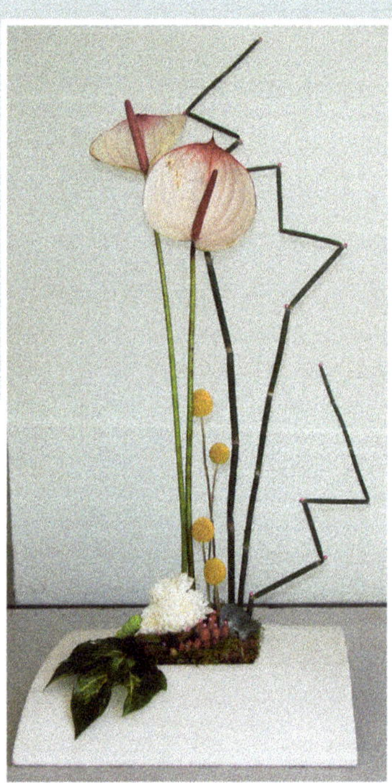

Techniques. Shadowing, framing, terracing, linear, graduating, rolling.

The parallel design

PRODUCE CUT TO DESIRED LENGTH

- ❑ 3 anthurium
- ❑ 7 mini gerbera
- ❑ 5 carnations
- ❑ 3 stems hypericum berries

FOLIAGE

- ❑ 1 stem solidaster
- ❑ 7 medium fatsia leaves
- ❑ 7 phormium leaves
- ❑ 3 black aspidistra leaves
- ❑ 3 stems black bamboo (cut into various lengths)
- ❑ 4 to 5 stems steel grass (threading the hypericum berries through)

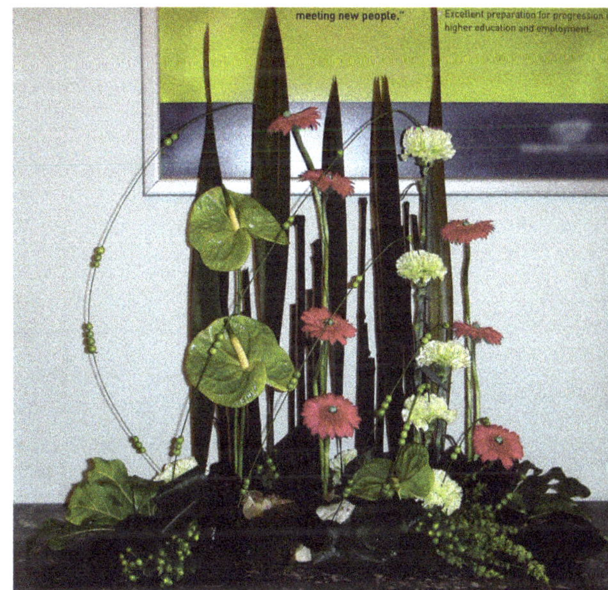

Long low Parallel

SUNDRIES

- ❑ 1 small rectangle tray
- ❑ 1 block wet oasis (horizontally placed and taped in for added support)
- ❑ 20 small mossing pins
- ❑ Colour headed pins for inserting into gerbera heads

METHOD

1. Place wet oasis onto tray and secure well with added florist tape in 3 equal distances.
2. Start with the fatsia, placing equally around and balanced onto the base of the oasis.
3. Add your phormium vertically, together with the various lengths of bamboo.
4. Cut the aspidistra leaf in half and fold to a roll, place pin inside and fasten to the oasis (you may need more pins), equally placed to balance the design.

5. Place anthurium, gerbera and carnations in place at vertical positions.
6. Start to thread the hypericum (1 stem) berries through the steel grass carefully, leaving spaces between each berry.
7. Place steel grass to oasis and overlap horizontally.
8. Finish off by placing colour headed pins into design.
9. Use the solidaster as a filler in gaps and by the side of the design.
10. Additionally with the rest of the hypericum.

Place in a prominent position or by a wall • Alternative flowers can be used • Refer to wiring techniques and image

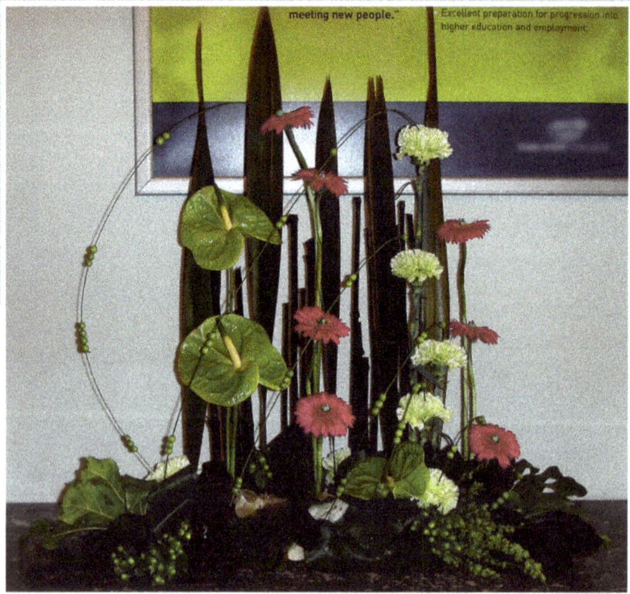

Techniques. Semi-caging, stapling foliage, terracing, threading, wiring

Contemporary decor

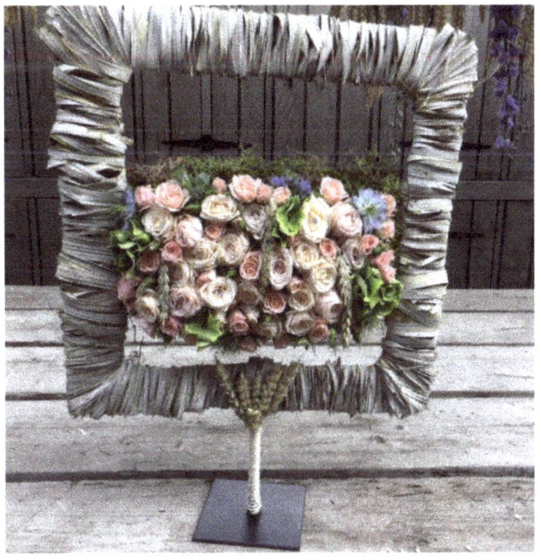

Contemporary table display

PRODUCE

- ❑ 3 to 4 stems spray pale pink & cream roscs cut into 5 inches
- ❑ 1 bloom of hydrangea (cut from 1 stem)
- ❑ A touch of blue (floral optional)

FOLIAGE

- ❑ 7 to 8 stems of dry grasses (optional variety)
- ❑ 4 to 5 dry long leaves of either grasses or phormium as an alternative
- ❑ ½ box of sphagnum moss
- ❑ Small moss pins

SUNDRIES

- ❑ Some coloured crystal headed pins (optional)
- ❑ 1 square hollow metal frame with stand (specialist supply)
- ❑ 1 hot glue gun and glue (training required for use here)
- ❑ 2 long green or black wooden 5mm sticks
- ❑ 1 block of wet oasis
- ❑ Florist tape

METHOD

1. Start with gluing at the base of the square metal frame (not the stand)
2. With a weave in and out method and over, use the glue gun, and place a dot form of glue as you go so the foliage stays secure.
3. Add as you go, join in the leaves by gluing carefully (so as not to burn your fingers).
4. Press slowly to get it secured to the other leaves.
5. By doing this method make sure you cover the mechanics.

6. Continue to do the weave in and out and over method, concentrating on the corners (by covering as much as you can in a tidy fashion), gluing at the same time.
7. To add the sticks, lay the frame down and balance the sticks so that a block of wet oasis can fit in between.
8. With sharp scissors, cut to size leaving ½ inch either side for anchoring to the frame (for security).
9. Place one stick into frame carefully ½ inch in) and glue.
10. Do the same for the other end, and check it is well balanced and level. Secure further with glue.
11. Continue with the other stick in the same way. (Leave a gap so the wet oasis fits firmly in, see attached photo.)
12. Tape round at both ends and secure to the sticks.

CONSTRUCTION

13. Add a layer of the moss to the whole side of 1 side, securing the moss to the oasis with the pins, cover the sides too.
14. Turn the display around and add some moss around the perimeter (1 inch) to the wet oasis.
15. You should have a rectangle gap within the oasis.
16. With your roses add to the design. And form an equal colour balance.
17. Continue to add the hydrangea (you may need to wire a few florets here).
18. For interest add 1 or 2 glass beads and/or heads of crystal headed pins (optional).
19. Pick up the design and place on a detachable stand. You can cover the stand with cream string (optional).

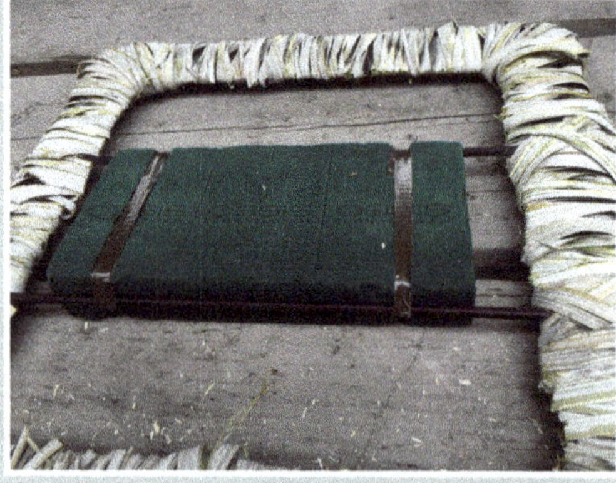

Techniques. Wedging, taping, winding

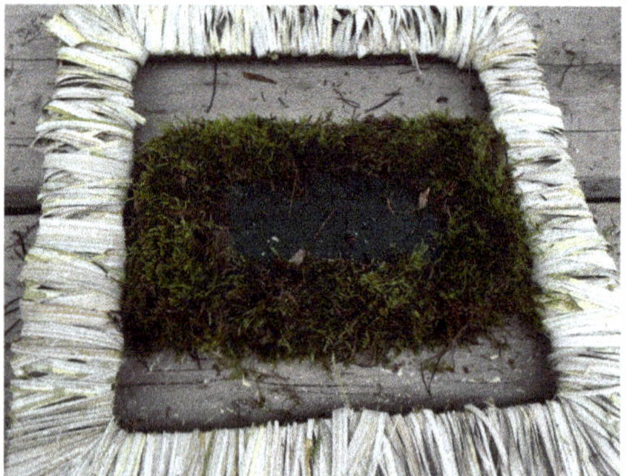

Techniques. Mossing, pinning

Health and safety precautions • Refer to wiring techniques and image • Place in a prominent display area or on a dining table • Alternative flowers can be used

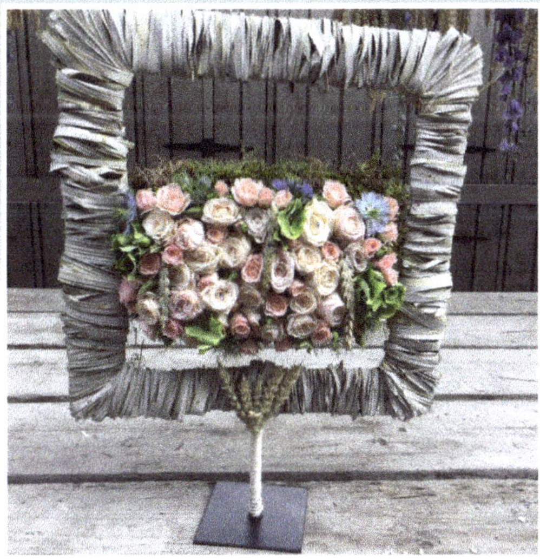

Techniques. Winding, basing, wiring, gluing, feathering, grouping of hydrangea blooms, wedging, wrapping of string on base

**Made at an advanced workshop*

Contemporary parallel

PRODUCE

- ❑ 2 anthuriums
- ❑ 7 craspedia
- ❑ 3 dianthus (carnations)
- ❑ 1 stem chrysanthemum (Kermit)

FOLIAGE

- ❑ 5 stems black bamboo (cut into various lengths)
- ❑ 3 phormium leaves
- ❑ 3 galax leaves
- ❑ Variegated euonymus, half stem (from a medium 10-inch length) cut into small 2 to 3 inch pieces
- ❑ 2 or 3 medium leaves ivy

SUNDRIES

- ❑ 1 rectangle clay low level trough
- ❑ 2 blocks of wet oasis foam
- ❑ Moss
- ❑ Mossing pins for moss

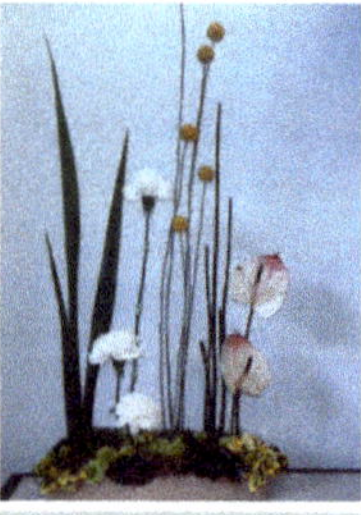

Contemporary parallel

METHOD

1. Firmly place wet oasis into container.
2. Cut excess oasis leaving 1 inch above the trough.
3. Start with placing the back area, place the phormium to one side, cut into various lengths.
4. Place your flower produce in the same way, about 2 inches apart horizontally.
5. Continue with the craspedia, snake grass and anthurium in the same manner.
6. For the base, apply the euonymus in corners, galax leaves in between and Kermit slightly vertically. Continue to fill your design with the rest of the foliage.
7. Add the moss to fill gaps, and secure with the moss pins.

Place in a prominent area • Alternative flowers can be used and refer to image for guided length of flowers • This design can be various lengths and sizes

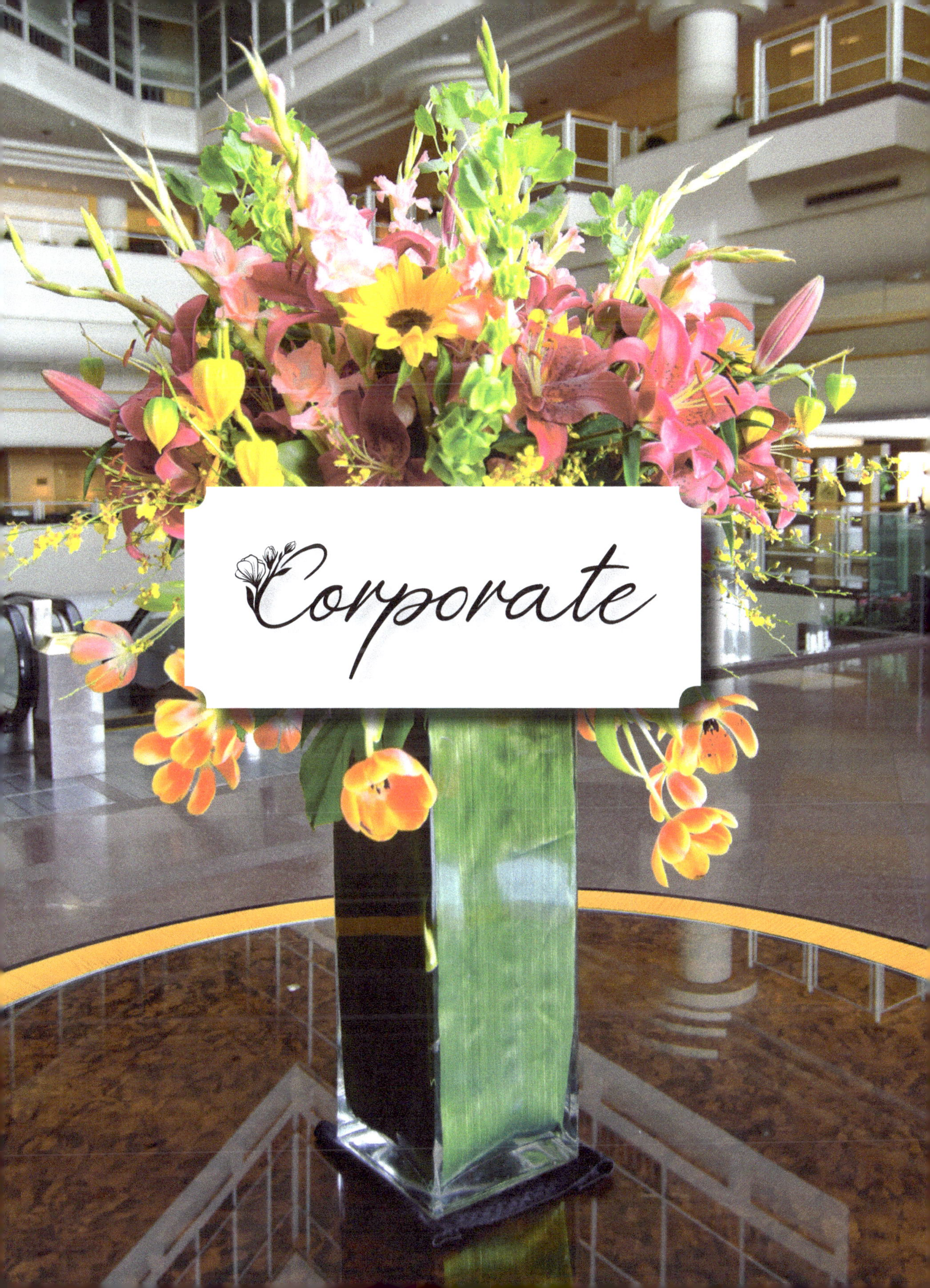
Corporate

Global foliage sphere

Textured sphere

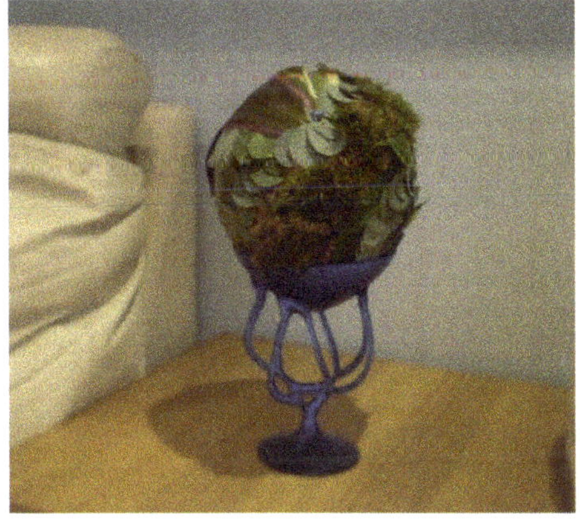

Foliage only design

Techniques. Texture Grouping, layering, pave, pinning, terracing

FOLIAGE

- ❑ 3 stems eucalyptus (baby blue)
- ❑ ¼ box of moss
- ❑ 2 Variegated cordyline leaves (red if possible)
- ❑ 1 stem variegated euonymus
- ❑ 2 stems green cordyline

SUNDRIES

- ❑ Display vase (round / cupped and slightly dipped in)
- ❑ 1 large wet oasis sphere ball
- ❑ Pins

METHOD

1. Soak the oasis ball in a bucket of water.
2. Lift out when fully covered and allow to stand for a few minutes.
3. Place onto a vase for support, while designing.
4. Start by taking leaves off the eucalyptus and pin on at a slight angle. Continue around the ball and meet up with the start. Use your cordyline and add this vertically next to the eucalyptus.
5. Adding the euonymus and variegated cordyline as you start to cover the sphere.
6. Fill in the larger gaps with moss and distribute the moss in areas to create a well balanced effect. Refer to image.

Place in a prominent position • Alternative foliage can be used

Front facing pedestal

PRODUCE CUT TO DESIRED LENGTH

- ❑ 3 stems phalaenopsis orchids
- ❑ 9 anthurium
- ❑ 3 cabbage
- ❑ 5 zantedeschia (green goddess)
- ❑ 3 strelitzia (birds of paradise)

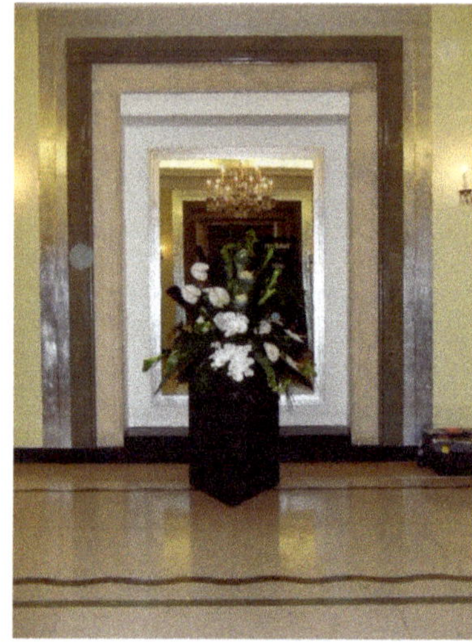

Pedestal at Claridge's Hotel

FOLIAGE

- ❑ 9 aspidistra leaves (green)
- ❑ 5 moluccella bells of Ireland
- ❑ 5 large palms stems' leaves
- ❑ 5 fish tail stems' leaves

SUNDRIES

- ❑ 1 large pedestal bowl
- ❑ 4 large wet oasis foams (pre-soaked)
- ❑ Florist tape (for anchoring the oasis to the bowl)
- ❑ Wire 74 gauge
- ❑ Wire made pins (74 gauge wire, bent in half, to make large pin sticks)
- ❑ Wooden thin sticks
- ❑ 6 metres lime green design wire (cut into 3)
- ❑ Oasis fix
- ❑ 1 or 2 large frog's legs

METHOD PREPARATION FOR THE PEDESTAL BOWL

Note: This is the most important part of the construction.

1. Soak the oasis in a bucket of water. Then remove and allow to stand for a few minutes.
2. Hold your pedestal bowl.

3. Place a large flog leg with some oasis fix to the bowl. You can do 2 if you wish (1 either side).
4. Press firmly down to secure well.
5. Cut ¼ off the 2 blocks.
6. Then add the 2 blocks of oasis side by side in a vertical position.
7. Pressing down firmly into bowl.
8. Fill the gaps with the extra oasis.
9. Tape up well, going underneath the bowl too, in a criss-cross fashion.
10. Once in place, secure with either thin wooden sticks, or 74 gauge wire folded in half (creating a U-shape).
11. Place the pins in the oasis by the join of the oasis, at 1 inch from the meeting point of the oasis.
12. Continue to place the sticks right through the central part of the oasis (horizontally) to support the oasis further.
13. Once the oasis has been secured in the bowl place to one side.

CONSTRUCTION OF THE FLOWERS

14. First start with the foliage.
15. The strelitzia first at the central top back, by placing next to each other with 2 to 3 inch gaps.
16. Then add the palms, sides left and right and central (facing you) by inserting the stems at a slight angle facing up into the oasis. Again one next to each other as above, creating a symmetrical design.
17. The foliage should aim forward, which is what you want it to do.
18. Fill the rest with the other foliage and cut to size as you are graduating the foliage in length. You are aiming for a triangular shape in profile and front visually.
19. Stand back a few times to see the shape forming as you go, looking all directions.
20. Add the cabbages in first at the top, one in front of the other. Going down the oasis. And you may need to cut to size here.
21. Then next to the cabbages add the zantedeschia (green goddess) in the same manner.
22. Continue to add the anthurium in the same way on the other side.
23. Place the anthurium opposite the rope placement to one side and add it to the bottom of the bowl (refer to picture) as you have done on the top, one in front of the other. So you are looking at it and have created an asymmetrical placement (refer to the picture).
24. Do this for the zantedeschia also (not forgetting to cut to size (e.g. smaller, medium, long)).

25. Add your phalaenopsis orchids aiming from the middle of the design down (to create a more graceful front symmetry, again cut to size).
26. With the rest of the foliage fill the gaps (don't forget to leave a gap at the back of the bowl for watering the display).
27. Make up 3 balls of design wire, leaving enough extra wire to place in the design at a balanced position.
28. Place the design onto a jardiniere or stand to suit its surroundings, best on a high stand.

Place design in churches, hotel foyers, wedding reception or other events • Alternative flowers and foliage can be used

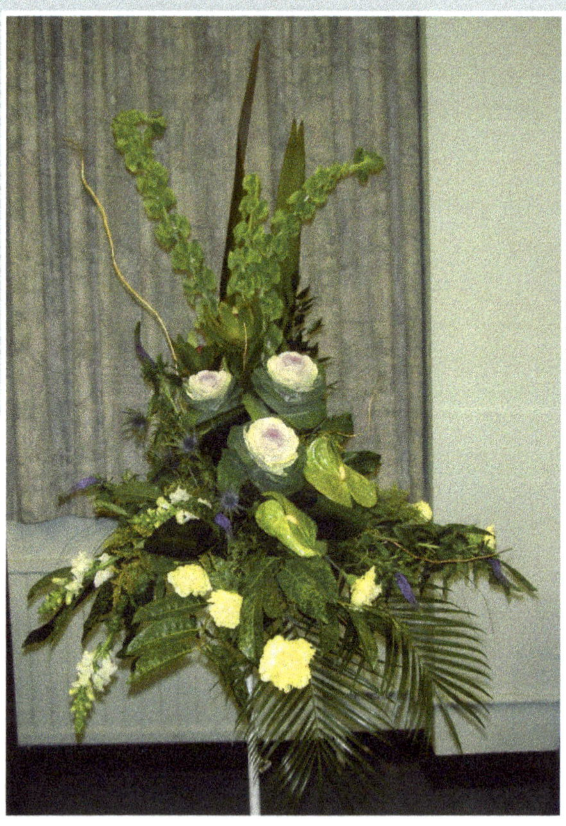

Front facing

Techniques. Radiate from centre front facing, stapling foliage, graduating, grouping of brassicas

Fireplace arrangement

PRODUCE

- ❑ 8 or 9 dendrobium stems
- ❑ 3 to 4 cymbidium orchids, stems cut in half

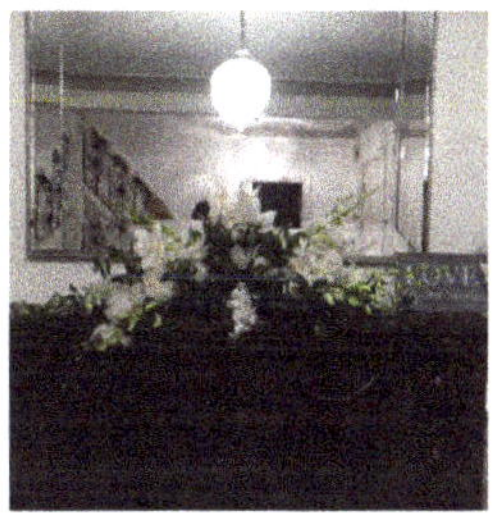

Long low decor design

FOLIAGE

- ❑ 8 long stems of soft ruscus, cut in half
- ❑ 4 long stems of eucalyptus, cut in half

SUNDRIES

- ❑ 1 long low small tray
- ❑ 1 block wet oasis foam soaked and allowed to stand for 5 to 6 minutes.
- ❑ Florist tape

METHOD

1. Place the wet oasis to the tray.
2. Secure both ends (about 2 inches in from the ends with florist tape, going underneath the tray also).
3. Start to place the ruscus in a horizontal way to the sides. The same for the eucalyptus.
4. Place the other foliage in the centre facing you, and do the same for the back part of the tray.
5. Fill the gaps vertically, cutting the foliage to size, to create a more diamond shape. Not forgetting the middle of the oasis.
6. Having foliage hanging facing down towards you. (Refer to picture.)
7. Apply the dendrobium equally around the design and making sure they are well secured in the oasis and balanced within the design (you may need to just stand back and view from a distance here).
8. Add the cymbidium orchids in the same fashion

Display on a fire surround or top table at an event
• Alternative flowers and foliage can be used

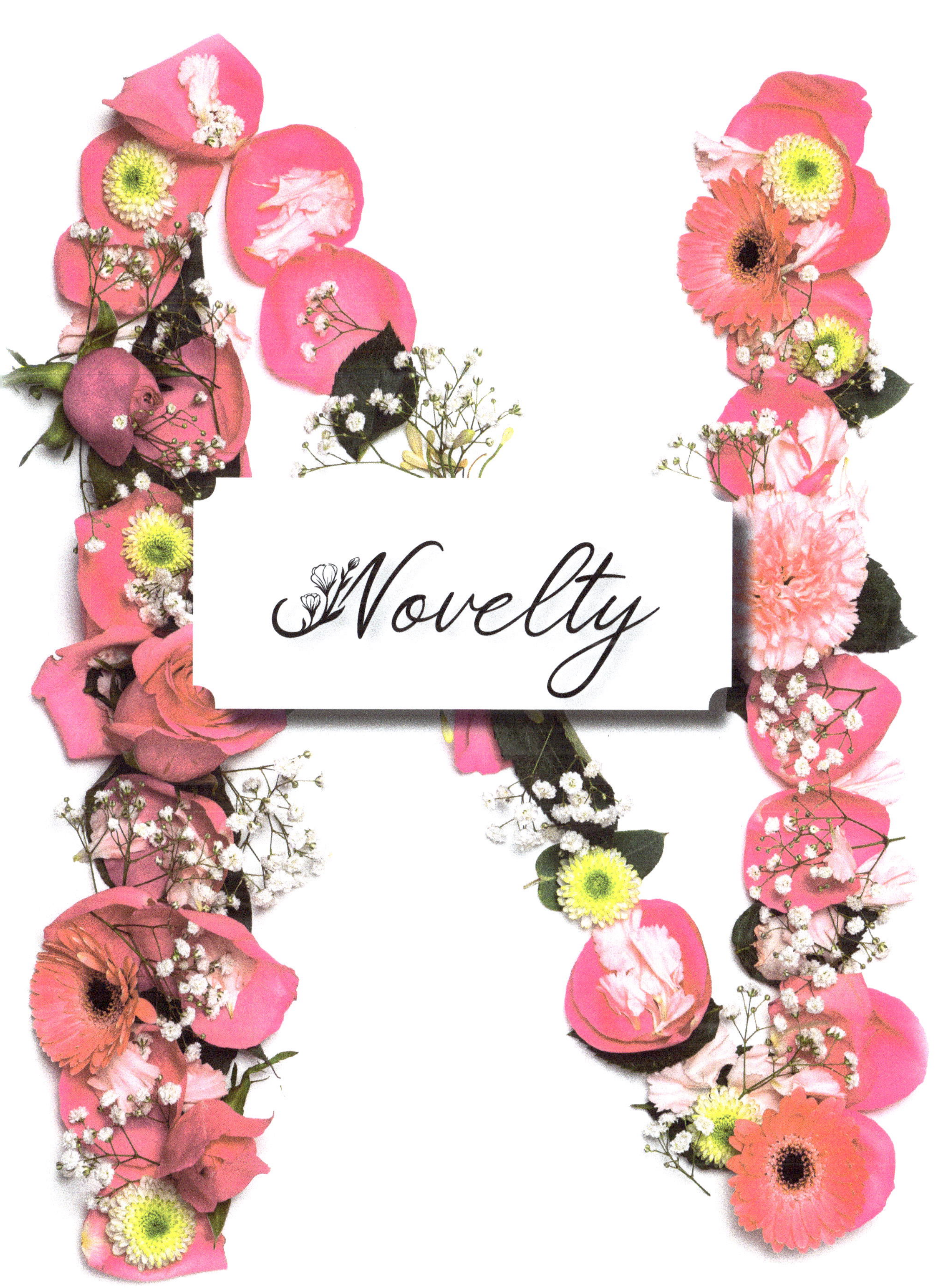
Novelty

Novelty cup

PRODUCE

- ❑ 2 stems chrysanthemum cut into 4 inches
- ❑ 6 stems of broom

FOLIAGE

- ❑ 3 or 4 large branches of laurel
- ❑ 2 large branches of silver leaf (cineraria)

SUNDRIES

- ❑ 1 design block of wet oasis (carved to a coffee cup shape before soaking in a bucket of water)
- ❑ Coffee granules
- ❑ Pins

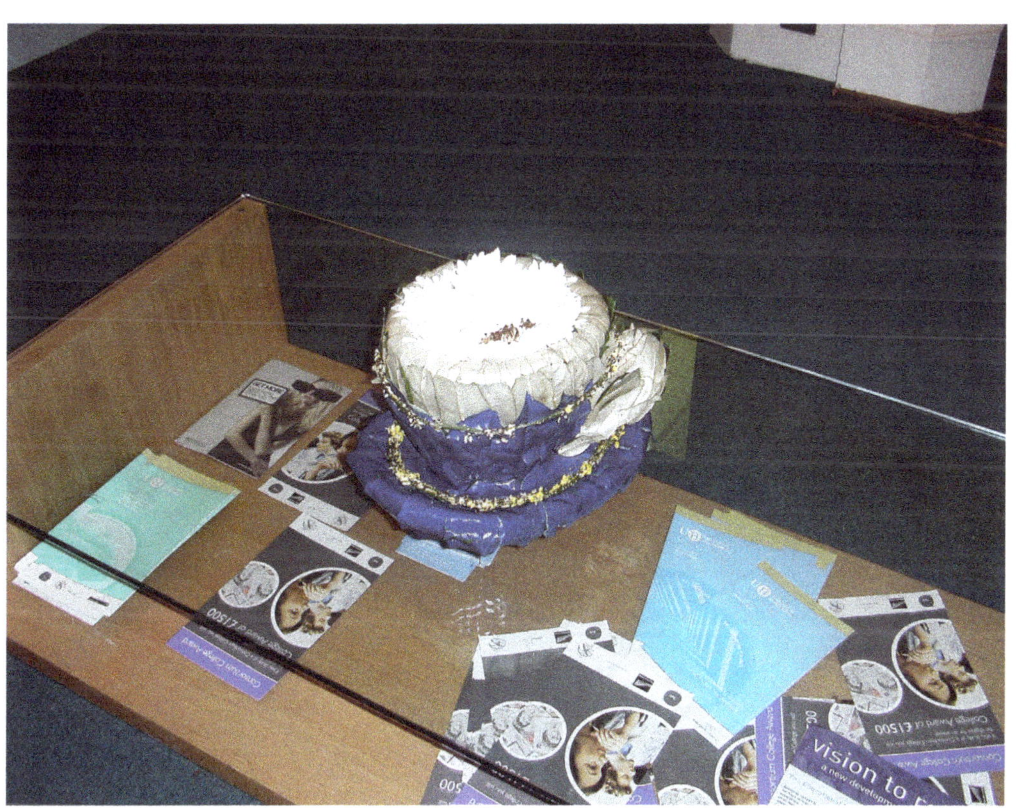

Novelty crockery

METHOD

1. Soak in a bucket and carefully lift out with both hands, allow to rest for 10 mins.
2. Start by pinning the laurel leaves on to the base in a vertical fashion by overlapping the leaves as you pin around the base. Cover the whole area.
3. Continue to work upwards and vertically around the design, making sure no pins can be visible.
4. At the top perimeter add the silver leaf in a vertical fashion and to the cup handle carefully.
5. Add the chrysanthemum in the central area.
6. Take 3 broom stems and wind with fine design wire to create a thicker stem. Do this 2 times.
7. Place the broom stems around the saucer of the design and pin in place to secure well. Do this to the cup also going through the cup handle.
8. Scatter coffee granules on to the chrysanthemums.

Place on a desk, or novelty events, tributes and corporate • Alternative foliage can be used • Techniques. Layering, pinning, plaiting, gluing.

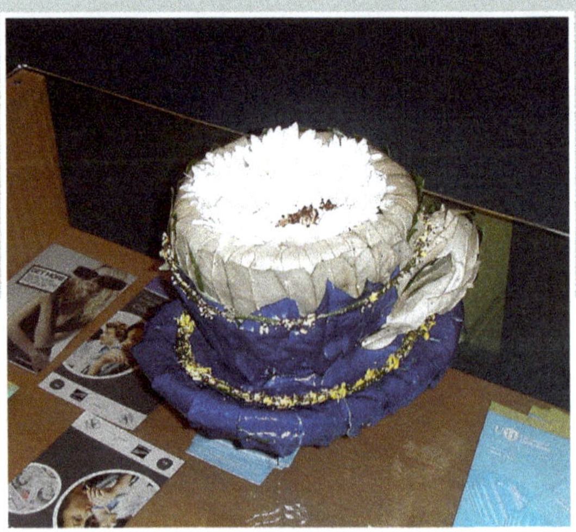

Novelty

Vegetative garden wreath

PRODUCE

- ❑ 1 small stem of spray carnation cut into 6 inches
- ❑ 1 small stem of spray aster September flower cut into 6 inches
- ❑ 1 stem limonium (statice) cut into 6 inches
- ❑ 1 small stem of spray chrysanthemum (Kermit) cut into 6 inches

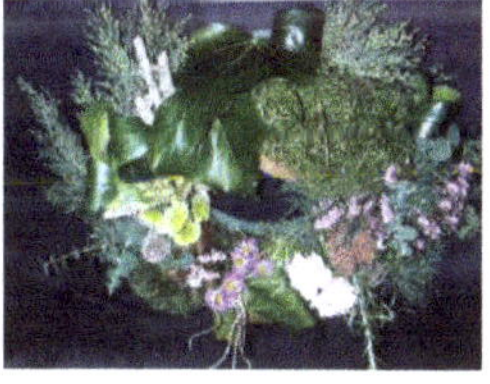

A garden wreath

FOLIAGE CUT INTO 8 INCHES

- ❑ 2 or 3 small individual ivy leaves
- ❑ 1 stem eucalyptus
- ❑ A handful of moss
- ❑ 6 variegated laurel leaves
- ❑ 1 small branch of conifer
- ❑ 1 small branch of rosemary
- ❑ 3 to 6 bark stems
- ❑ 5 to 6 small cones wired with 74 wire gauge

SUNDRIES

- ❑ 1 wet oasis open 16 inch wreath ring
- ❑ Small mossing pins

METHOD

1. Soak the wreath well in a bucket until fully covered.
2. Start to create your garden by adding the conifer in 3 areas of the ring, covering the bottom too. (This can be done vertically.)
3. Add the moss in the same way, using moss pins to secure in place.
4. Then the eucalyptus.
5. Roll the ivy leaves and place in the gaps, secure with the moss pins.
6. Add the carnation spray in 1 or 2 areas.

7. Add the aster next to the ivy.
8. Continue to add the limonium.
9. Fill the gaps with the chrysanthemum (Kermits).
10. Place the rosemary between the small cones.
11. Then add the bark stems.

Place on a themed garden table or garden event • Alternative foliage can be used, refer to wiring techniques and image.

Textured hollow wreath

PRODUCE

- ❑ 4 spray roses
- ❑ 1 stem chrysanthemum (Kermit)
- ❑ 1 stem chrysanthemum (dark pink)

FOLIAGE

- ❑ ¼ stem from (ten inches) rosemary
- ❑ 3 stems snake grass (cut up into 2 or 3 inches)
- ❑ 3 stems steel grass cut in half
- ❑ ½ stems eucalyptus (baby blue)
- ❑ 2 or 3 medium leaf ivy
- ❑ 1 leaf length cordyline (cut into 1 inch cubes)
- ❑ 1 stem silver leaf
- ❑ 3 stems hypericum berries (purple)
- ❑ ¼ branch of a medium branch of laurel
- ❑ ¼ stem black hypericum berry

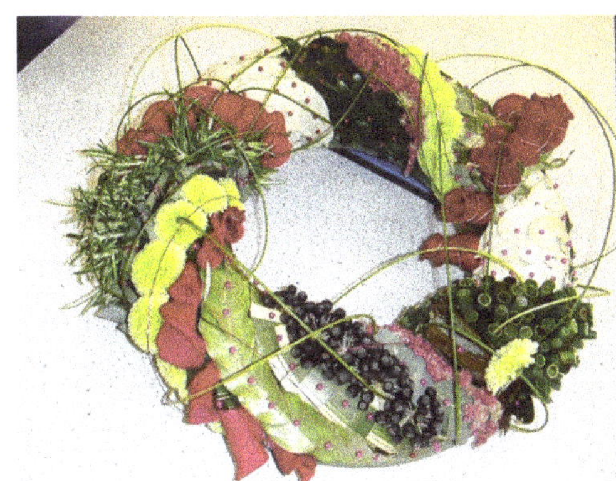

Textured Wreath

SUNDRIES

- ❑ Colour headed pin heads
- ❑ 1 oasis ring wreath 15 inches.

METHOD

1. Wet oasis ring naturally in a bucket of water.
2. Condition all produce and cut to required lengths.
3. Start with the laurel leaves (only) and start to place them diagonally onto the wreath and pin into place with one pin either end.
4. Overlap the second leaves and continue the pinning, covering one pin, so only one pin is showing.
5. Continue to apply your materials diagonally with your choice of placement in design.

6. For the snake grass place into oasis (1 inches) vertically with aim to continue the diagonal shape.
7. Continue to place your roses and other produce, pinning the foliage also. Apply the 6 steel grass by placing into oasis 1 inch and bring over the design by a diagonal movement and place further down the design to give the weaved effect.

Making sure you cover all oasis and mechanics • Refer to image • Place on a desired area for show • Alternative flowers can be used • Refer to image

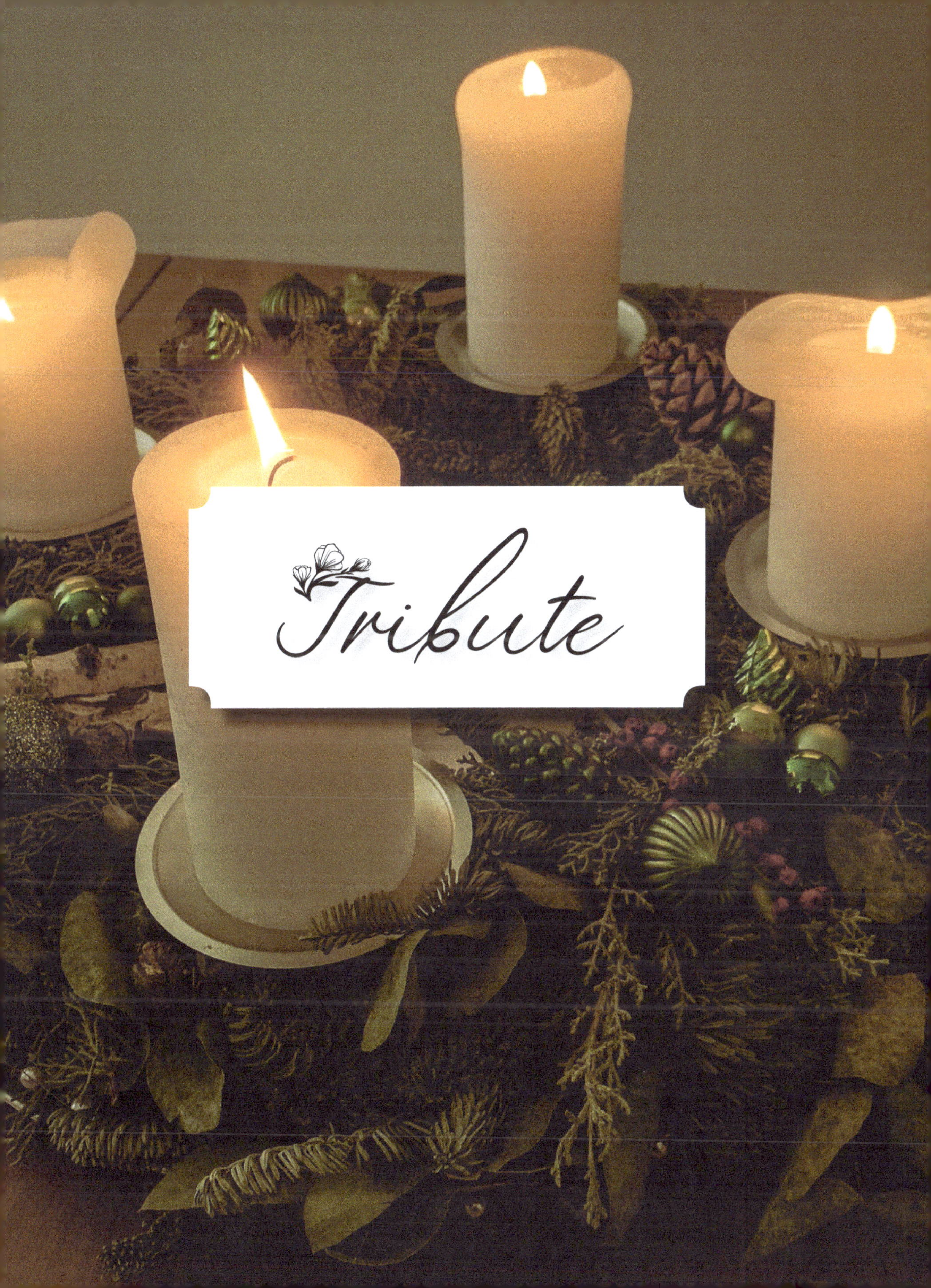
Tribute

Novelty Anchor tribute

PRODUCE

- ❑ 20 stems double white chrysanthemums (for basing)
- ❑ 5 gerbera
- ❑ 1 stem chrysanthemum (for spray)
- ❑ 5 veronica
- ❑ 1 stem spray dianthus (carnations)
- ❑ Refer to international heart tribute for length of flowers.

FOLIAGE

- ❑ 2 stems leather leaf leaves
- ❑ 1 stem eucalyptus (parvi)

SUNDRIES

- ❑ 1½ metres yellow rope (made into a continuous link)
- ❑ 1 Anchor wet oasis base
- ❑ 2 mts pre folded in (overlap fashion) ribbon
- ❑ Large mossing pins
- ❑ 1 medium Le-Bump attachment
- ❑ 74 wire for rope to attach to design

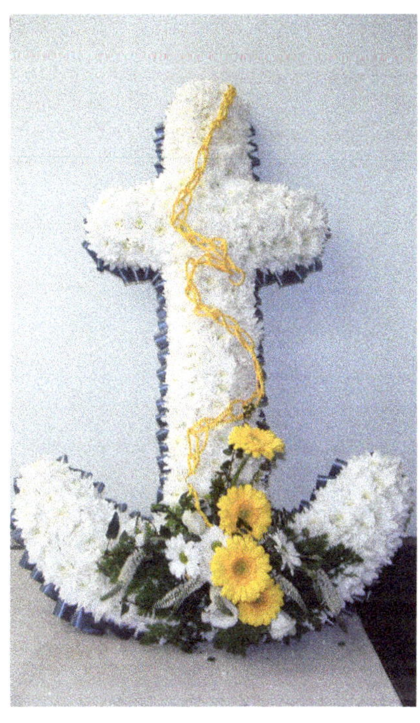

Anchor

METHOD

1. Soak the anchor wet oasis well until fully covered.
2. Trim the inside and outside perimeter by removing the corners. This to create a smoother edge.
3. Place Le-Bump in place (central).
4. Start by placing ribbon on the bottom of the base, just before the tray or hard base ends on the wet oasis; attach the ribbon with the moss pins in 1 inch placements.
5. Continue round the whole anchor and secure well at joining point.

BASING METHOD

6. Cut the smaller blooms from the double chrysanthemum and place them at the base of the design, slightly overlapping with the ribbon (this to hide the pins).
7. Continue round the anchor trying to keep the same size bloom all round.
8. Next layer, apply the more medium bloom (this you insert into wet oasis and leave ½ inch out of the oasis, so you are starting to create a cushion effect by graduating it upwards for the design).
9. Continue around the anchor.
10. The larger blooms for the rest of the design and keeping to a regimented line for the central part.
11. For the spray, you cut the foliage to size (6 to 7 inches for the leather leaf) and insert to the side of the Le-bump. Insert the smaller lengths left over to the top and bottom of the spray. And the very small bits of the leaf within the Le bump.
12. Continue to add the rest of the foliage, in various small, medium and larger pieces so the Le-bump looks well balanced and slight diamond shape (as illustrated in the picture).
13. Add your gerbera first, taller at the top and not overlapping the foliage leaf.
14. Add the rest of the gerbera and the spray chrysanthemum to its side.
15. Continue to place the carnations to the design, again in the diamond shape format.
16. Add the veronica to the sides and equally balanced.
17. Add the rope, by attaching this with some wire, by twisting the wire round until firmly secure, insert the wire (5 inches to the wet oasis).

Alternative flowers can be used • Refer to wiring techniques and international Heart tribute • Can be used as a tribute or novelty

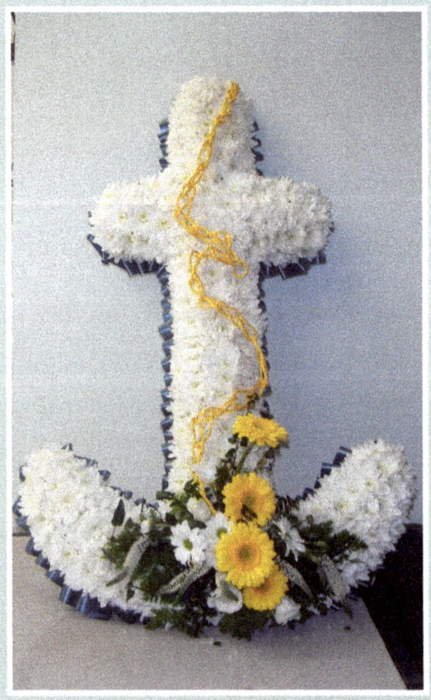

Novelty tribute

Techniques. Basing, tying, knotting, grouping, pleating of ribbon, wiring.

International heart wreath

PRODUCE

- ❑ 1 stem lily (preferably with 2 open heads cut into 6 inches)
- ❑ 9 pink gerbera cut into 5 inches
- ❑ 2 stems pink chrysanthemums cut into 4 inches
- ❑ 3 stems white chrysanthemums cut into 4 inches

FOLIAGE

- ❑ ¼ stem eucalyptus (baby blue)

SUNDRIES

- ❑ 1 16-inch heart shaped wet oasis pad

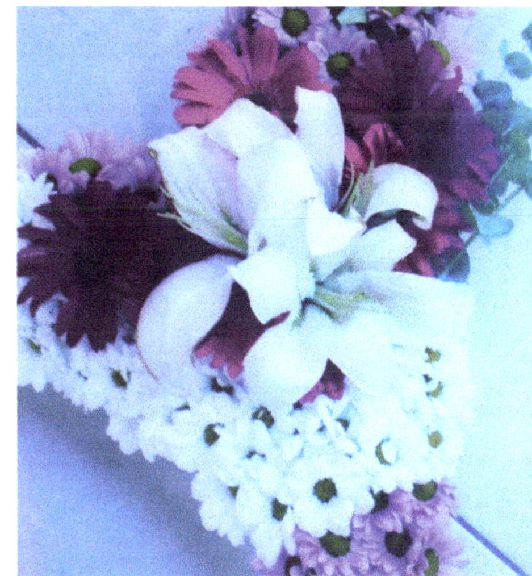

Heart wreath

METHOD

1. Soak oasis in a bucket.
2. Prepare the heart, by curving the corners of the pad with a small florist knife. Hand smooth the edges.
3. Start by placing the pink chrysanthemum into base about (1 inch into oasis) from the corner and covering the base of the pad. Continue to create a triangular area.
4. Adding the white chrysanthemum to follow, and bring up into the pad so you cover some of the middle oasis. Additionally, by continual placement of the chrysanthemum across the pad, cover another corner.
5. Unite the pink chrysanthemum and continue this until all 3 corners are covered and you have a central gap in which to place your other produce.
6. Place gerbera slightly above the chrysanthemum and work in a circular movement, so that all gerberas are around the heart.
7. Add the lily heads slightly higher so they are more prominent.
8. Finish with your eucalyptus to one side.

Designed for tributes & sympathy • Alternative flowers can be used

Moss hollow wreath

PRODUCE

- ❑ 1 small stem of cymbidium orchids

FOLIAGE

- ❑ ½ a box of sphagnum moss
- ❑ 1 small stem of blue spruce pine

SUNDRIES

- ❑ 20 Small moss pins
- ❑ 1 wet oasis foam wreath open ring 15 inches

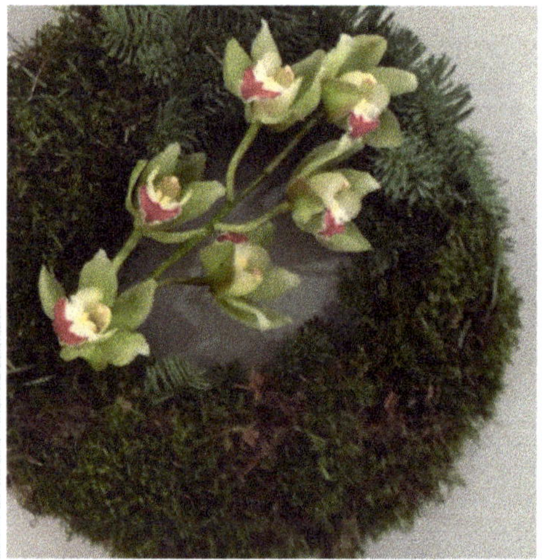

Christmas moss wreath

METHOD

1. Place the moss over the wreath ring to cover ¾ of it (but cover the bottom base of the ring with moss).
2. The other ¼ of the oasis add the blue spruce pine in a slight vertical fashion.
3. Add the cymbidium orchid to the opposite side of the design, so the cymbidium is facing the pine.
4. Insert into the oasis (1 inch).

Place as a tribute or door wreath (with added ribbon to attach to a door knocker) • Alternative flowers can be used

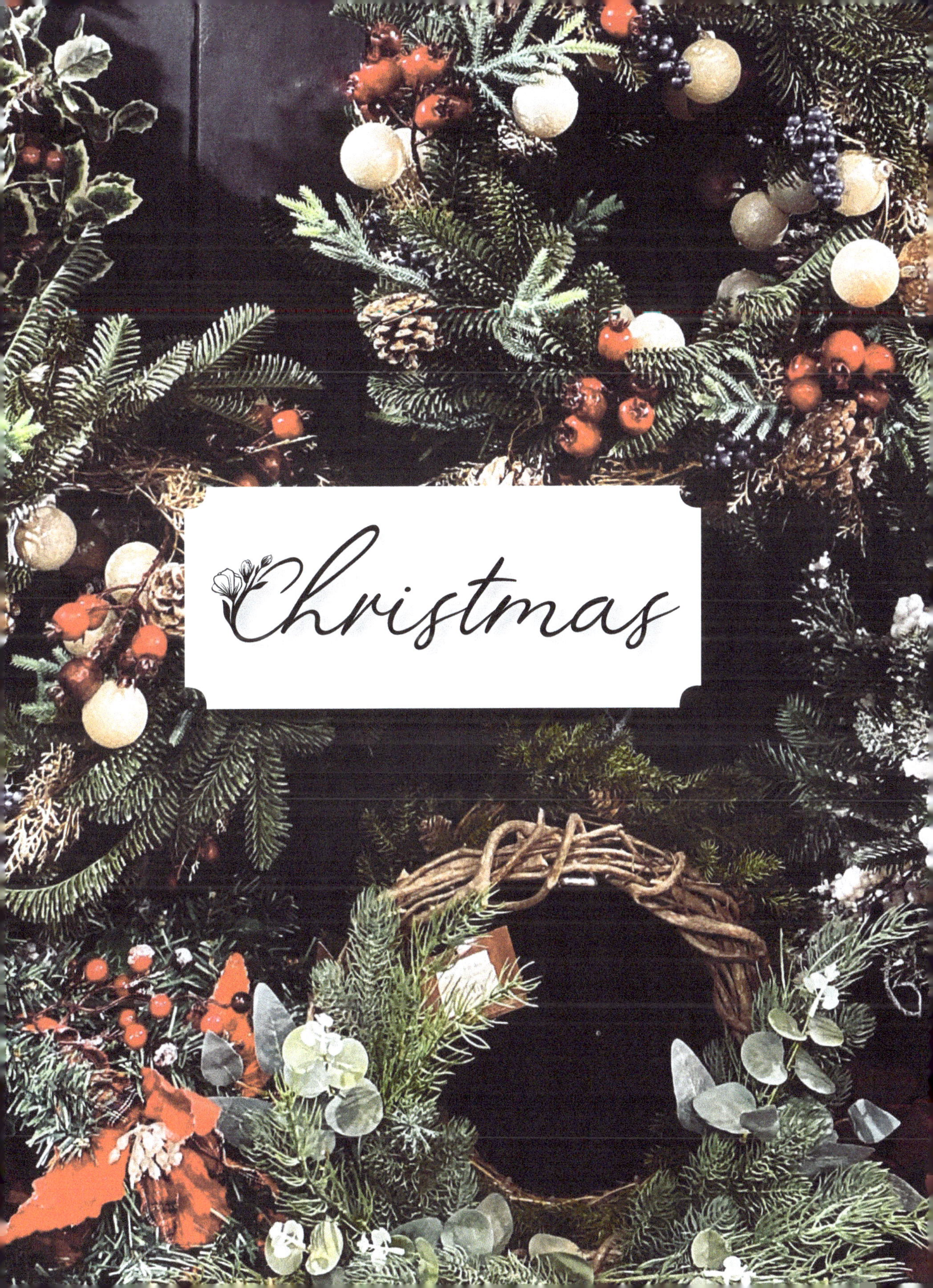
Christmas

Christmas candle

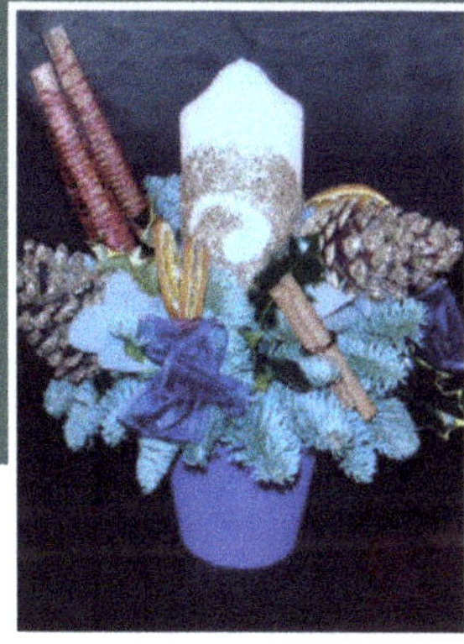

Christmas side table candle arrangement

FOLIAGE

- ❑ 1 small pine branch cut to 8 inches
- ❑ 1 small stem of holly cut to 8 inches

SUNDRIES

- ❑ 2 to 3 cones
- ❑ 1 or 2 cinnamon sticks
- ❑ 4 to 6 dried orange segments
- ❑ 1 candle
- ❑ ¼ wet oasis foam
- ❑ 1 small planter (designer's choice)
- ❑ Florist tape
- ❑ 74 gauge wire
- ❑ Design wire for cinnamon sticks

METHOD

1. Apply wet oasis to the planter.
2. Secure over the oasis with florist tape.
3. Start by cutting the pine to reasonable lengths to 7 to 10 inches.
4. Remove some of the pine needles from the bottom (this to be able to place into oasis more clearly).
5. Bend 3 to 4 wires in half.
6. Apply the wires to the candle base area (about ½ inch from the bottom of the candle.
7. Carefully tape round the wire and secure them equally around the candle.
8. Cut the wires to 5 inches.
9. Place the candle in the middle of the planter (in the oasis) firmly.
10. Start adding the pine at the bottom of the planter going round the whole area.
11. Continue to fill the oasis, and adding some holly to balance.
12. Wire the cones (by twisting the wire around the cone, leaving 3 inches spare (to place into oasis).
13. Continue to wire your sundries leaving enough wire to go into oasis and place equally around the design.
14. Wind the design wire around the cinnamon sticks. Secure safely.
15. Apply the cinnamon sticks into design.

Place on a Christmas table • Alternative foliage can be used • Refer to wiring techniques

Christmas garland

FOLIAGE

- ❑ Note, all foliage should be cut to the same size.
- ❑ 3 to 4 medium branches of blue spruce pine (cut the small individual pieces from each branch, and the joined pieces kept and cut together)
- ❑ 2 or 3 stems of eucalyptus (cut into small pieces from the stem, leaf size)
- ❑ 1 stem of green conifer (cut to small pieces the same as the eucalyptus).

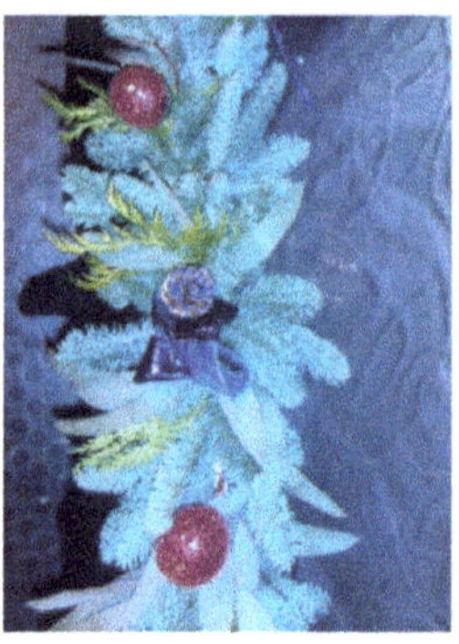

Christmas pine garlands

SUNDRIES

- ❑ Christmas baubles
- ❑ 1 to 2 metres of green rope to secure the pine to.
- ❑ 1 reel wire

METHOD

1. Take three pieces of pine and join with the reel wire, a few twists round; apply this to the star of the rope (foliage facing outwards).
2. Do the same for the other foliage and alternate the placements.
3. Continue to add the tree pieces of foliage in front of the previous pine (about 1 inch down) and twist the wire round the rope and pine together, going underneath the rope and over a few times with the reel wire. (Do not cut the reel wire at any stage of the formation of the garland.)
4. Continue until the middle of the rope.
5. Once in the middle, place the pine and eucalyptus guiding them in to face up and down in the central area leading to putting the foliage the other way onto the rope.
6. This will then have a format of the foliage being displayed with the same method as the first piece of pine (see the picture at the ends and middle).
7. To add the baubles' wire with 74 gauge wire, through the baubles' heads and twist wire together and then place some under the whole garland, by placing the wire in between the foliage and up facing the bauble.

8. Twist the wire around the bauble and secure well to the garland. Making sure the wire is hidden and safe.

Display on staircase, windowsill or have the garland display vertically
• Alternative foliage can be used • Refer to wiring techniques

Christmas Scented orange tree

PRODUCE

- ❑ 1 pack dried orange slices
- ❑ 1 small pack mini gold baubles
- ❑ 1 small stem of pine

SUNDRIES

- ❑ 1 mini small bowl
- ❑ 1 small frog's leg
- ❑ Potting tape
- ❑ ¼ inch oasis fix
- ❑ 1 small wet oasis Christmas cone
- ❑ 46 gauge wire for oranges and baubles

METHOD

1. Soak oasis Christmas cone in water, allow to soak naturally.
2. Remove when ready and allow to stand for 5 minutes.
3. Apply oasis fix to the middle of the bowl.
4. Add the frog's leg pressing firmly down.
5. Add your Christmas cone in the centre, and press firmly into the frog's leg.
6. Tape over the whole tree once, secured well with the tape.
7. Wire the oranges by placing the wire through the segment and looping over and twist to the longer piece of wire. Cut to size about 3 inches, the same process for the baubles.
8. Start to apply the small stems of pine around the base unwired. Refer to wiring techniques.

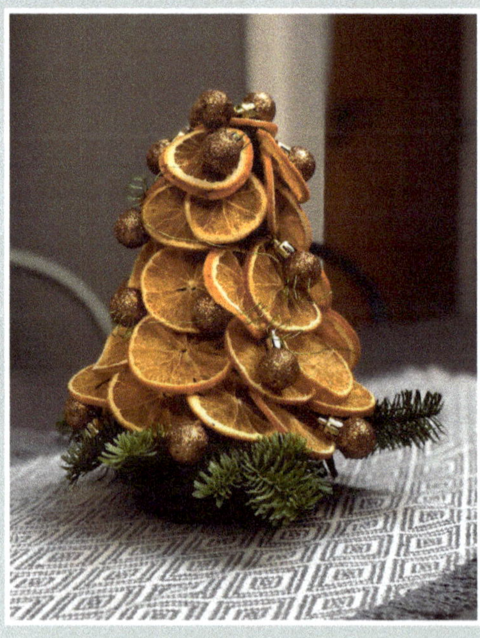

Christmas Scented orange tree

9. Add the orange slices around the base first and overlap the oranges.
10. Continue to the top, cutting the wire smaller according to the shape of the tree.
11. Add your baubles to decorate. Refer to image.

Position in a place of your choice • Can use alternative seasonal fruits and décor • Refer to wiring techniques.

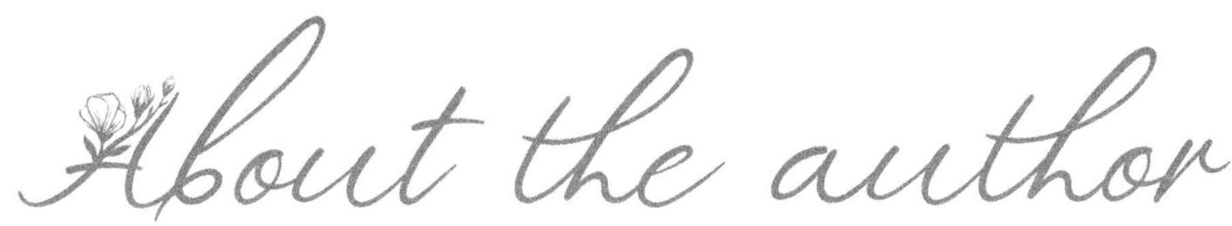

Creative in art, with a good understanding of the current and new trends that are moving the arts world forward.

Keen interest in all departments of the Arts industry.

Has a creative flair to show new enthusiasts the way forward to a new and rewarding Hobby or career in Floristry.

Never stop learning or give up your ambitions.

www.ingramcontent.com/pod-product-compliance
Lightning Source LLC
LaVergne TN
LVHW060628110826
845147LV00015B/957

* 9 7 8 1 9 1 4 1 9 5 2 6 6 *